A COACH'S GUIDE TO MAXIMIZING THE YOUTH SPORT EXPERIENCE

This book guides sport coaches, parents and administrators in creating a caring and task-involving sport climate that helps athletes perform their best and have an enjoyable and meaningful sport experience. It introduces the concept of a caring and task-involving climate and provides a "how to" guide to creating this climate in sport.

Firstly, this guide introduces the caring and task-involving climate and summarizes research highlighting its many benefits. Secondly, the five features of this climate are presented along with the reflective exercises for developing them within a team. Coaches will see strategies in action, sample conversations, and a variety of ways to implement the features of a caring and task-involving experience. By describing how it may be implemented and methods for overcoming possible challenges, this book finally highlights how parents and sport administrators can support the creation and preservation of caring and task-involving climates.

By helping teams develop caring climates that optimize athletes' sport experience and performance, this book is essential reading for coaches, sport administrators, parents, and sport psychology practitioners. It will also be of great interest to those who have minimal training in sport psychology, but who are involved in sport at many levels, such as youth and high school.

Mary Fry is a professor and Director of the Sport and Exercise Psychology Lab at the University of Kansas. A former coach and athlete, she has worked with coaches, across a variety of sports and skill levels, to help them maximize their athletes' sport experiences.

Lori Gano-Overway is an assistant professor in the Department of Kinesiology at James Madison University. She has worked in coach education for over 20 years studying the influence of the climate and consulting with coaches to create environments to support athletes' physical, psychological, and social development.

Marta Guivernau is an assistant professor in the Department of Sport Management at Kent State University and certified mental performance consultant. Her focus is on creating positive climates in sport to optimize the experience and lifespan development of all participants. She works with coaches, D1 teams and athletes on performance-related issues, psychological and socio-emotional wellbeing.

Mi-Sook Kim is a professor in the Department of Kinesiology at San Francisco State University. She has worked with competitive athletes including college athletes and professional golfers to enhance their mental performance. She also provides workshops for managers of corporations and coaches and parents in motivational strategies and psychological skills.

Maria Newton is an associate professor and director of graduate studies in the Department of Health, Kinesiology, and Recreation at the University of Utah. She is a Fellow with the Association for Applied Sport Psychology. She has over 50 publications largely centered on the impact and influence of the climate in relation to motivation. She is particularly interested in maximizing the experience of youth in both sport and exercise settings.

"As a coach, this book is a roadmap that outlines what I aspire to be. The authors clearly demonstrate the value of creating a caring sports climate and provide excellent examples for achieving that aim. While underpinned by decades of research, the content is refreshingly accessible and keeps the focus exactly where it belongs – on youth athletes and enriching their experiences in sport. This book is at the front of my bookshelf and is required reading for coaching staff and parents."

– Gabe Downey, Head Diving Coach, University of Kansas

"Athletes today expect coaches to know them well enough to care and respect them. They also want to be involved in creating and implementing tactics and techniques in their sport. This book helps you meet their expectations. It provides theories, methods, and examples from coaches and players to do everything from interacting effectively with your athletes and involving them in a team where athletes care about and support each other. This is a *go to* source when looking for answers to coaching questions."

– Jay Coakley, Ph.D., Professor Emeritus, University of Colorado

A COACH'S GUIDE TO MAXIMIZING THE YOUTH SPORT EXPERIENCE

Work Hard, Be Kind

Mary Fry
Lori Gano-Overway
Marta Guivernau
Mi-Sook Kim
Maria Newton

Routledge
Taylor & Francis Group

NEW YORK AND LONDON

First published 2020
by Routledge
52 Vanderbilt Avenue, New York, NY 10017

and by Routledge
2 Park Square, Milton Park, Abingdon, Oxon, OX14 4RN

Routledge is an imprint of the Taylor & Francis Group, an informa business

Library of Congress Cataloging-in-Publication Data
A catalog record for this title has been requested

ISBN: 978-0-367-25413-1 (hbk)
ISBN: 978-0-367-25415-5 (pbk)
ISBN: 978-0-429-28768-8 (ebk)

Typeset in Bembo
by Newgen Publishing UK

This book is dedicated to those coaches who devote their time and energy to creating positive sport experiences for their athletes.
Mary: To Andy, Jared, Lindsey & Ollie, for their love and inspiration.
Lori: To Ken and the Gano-Overway clan, for their patience, encouragement and support.
Mi-Sook: To Chungsoo, Eujean and Sujean, for sparking my curiosity and courage.
Maria: Mary, Joe and Scout for being my most favorite playing partners.
Marta: To Jaume, Julia, Marc & Sara, for being the best team I could ever wish for.

CONTENTS

PREFACE

Yesterday we heard from a grandmother who was distraught about her grandson's experience on his youth baseball team. She had gone to watch his team play in a tournament, and was appalled that immediately after one game the grandson's team was out on the field running as punishment for their mistakes in the game. In addition, the athletes were banned from going anywhere near family or friends who had come to see them play. After they played the second game later in the day, again the athletes were punished by having to do push-ups, etc. for every mistake. This grandmother has no training in the field of sport psychology, but she knew this was not good for kids and not what sport should be about. She resented the fact that she could not give her grandson a hug and share the sport experience with him, and that the entire experience, created by the coaches, was so negative. She recognized how messed up youth sport can be. Unfortunately, we hear these stories about negative sport environments daily.

Coaches who create negative environments as described above are likely not doing so because they are trying to harm young athletes. Many have only had exposure to this kind of sport environment and may genuinely believe they are helping athletes develop discipline, character, and athletic skill. The thing is, this coaching behavior should never happen today because we know so much about how harmful it is for athletes, and how a positive approach helps athletes thrive and reach their potential. How can there continue to be so many negative environments out there in sport when we know so much about how to help athletes develop their skills and have great sport experiences? We do not have the answer to this question; it seems like the wealth of sport psychology research should be at work everywhere we turn, in every youth sport program, in every swim lesson, in all physical activity settings across the land. But it is not. Clearly there is much work to be done to move sport psychology from research to practice.

A friend of ours, Sandi Mitchell, describes her work as a corporate consultant as being all about helping employers "connect the dots" between their behaviors and the impact they have on employees. In a similar vein, what we are attempting to do with this book is help coaches connect the dots, to receive guidance in applying sport psychology research into their real-life coaching. While we briefly describe theory and research, the essence of this book is about helping coaches understand the key role they play in creating a positive climate for their athletes. Coaches are difference-makers, they change athletes' lives. We could not be more convinced that, together, coaches could help achieve world peace. Okay, we said that for affect, but we are sincere in our belief that coaches' impact can be awe-inspiring and make a difference in the lives of many athletes. We have written this book to help coaches and others who are trying to help sport become all it can be for young athletes. We are on this journey together.

PART I

Introduction

1

A CARING AND TASK-INVOLVING CLIMATE

The Key to Maximizing Sport Performance and Experience

Highlights

- Coaches play a major role in helping their athletes reach their potential.
- When coaches help athletes define success based on their effort and improvement, athletes reap many physical, mental, and emotional benefits.
- Coaches are key players in creating a caring and task-involving climate on their teams that trickles down and sets the state for great sport experiences.

I was one of those kids that participated in every sport imaginable and as a result I've had many coaches over the years. It is interesting to realize, good or bad, all of them had a tremendous impact on me. I recall Chuck who coached my community softball team when I was 12. He was a 'man's man' – a big muscular guy with a bushy mustache. I would ride my bike as fast as I could to practice because he treated us like we were the San Francisco Giants. For those 2 hours we were his universe. Practices were planned out to the minute and every single drill was focused on effort and improvement. Every dropped ball (and there were plenty) was an opportunity to learn and improve. Every player – both good and bad – got all of Chuck's attention and expertise. All of us – a pretty ragged bunch I imagine – were his Giants and he treated us with so much respect that to this day I still stand a little straighter and am proud of that team. I went on to receive some of the 'best' coaching in the United States and I can say that nobody ever quite lived up to the caring and task-involving climate that Chuck created. I think it just goes to show that coaches matter at every level and at the heart of good coaching is the coaching climate.

Maria Newton

My first career goal was to become a female coach that would express care for female runners, and understand how the body changes their experience during puberty. As a competitive runner, I had only experienced ego-involving coaches who were only focused on my performance. Then one day Coach Kim came into my life; he was a coach who cared about all athletes and had their best interests in mind. He tried to look at things from his athletes' perspective and it made such a difference. He motivated the team to be the best student-athletes we could be, and he helped us thrive in both school and sport. He not only coached us in our sport but also helped us become the best people we could be.

Mi-Sook Kim

My dad was the main force behind me being active and participating in sports. He taught me to ski when I was 6, took my sister and me skating, swimming but most of all, he got us into hiking in the Pyrenees. He taught me endurance, pacing myself, persistence and to keep going beyond what I thought I could do. It was never about how high we could go but about completing the journey together. In school, it is not my coaches I recall most but my teammates. Thinking back though, I know my experience was ingrained by the atmosphere those coaches infused. My days were full of gymnastics, relays, basketball but also hours of unstructured play, dodgeball, jump rope and improvising games. The connections we built with each other last to this day. It was not until college that I realized that not everyone had a positive experience in sport and that success was often defined by being the best instead of being our best together. I was lucky to land at the Sport Psych program at Purdue, with great people that became best friends and a mentor who taught us about task-involving climates. Since then, I have been fortunate to work and learn from athletes and coaches to focus on helping reflect sports as they were for me when I was young.

Marta Guivernau Rojas

I really lucked out in middle school and high school in that I had coaches who cared about me as a person and motivated me to do my best. My Dad reinforced this notion that you always work hard and try to make yourself better. However, when I went to college, I learned that not all of my teammates and classmates had the same experience with coaches. They were yelled at for not performing well, pitted against one another, and did not have a good relationship with their coaches. These experiences made me realize that coaches really make a difference in the lives of athletes.

Lori Gano-Overway

When I graduated from college I was fortunate to walk right into a premium job as a tennis coach at a large school district in Texas. Whew, what a learning experience that was as I (the lone coach) began coaching the boys and girls' teams (over 50 athletes) with full fall and spring schedules. My goal was to help bring out the best in every athlete I coached, and I realized quickly that such an aim was tougher to deliver than I expected. As I look back now, I realize that I somehow instinctively knew that the keys to maximizing the sport experience for my athletes were directly tied to encouraging high effort; giving instructional feedback and noticing improvement; creating a team bond where all athletes felt connected; and deeply caring about each athlete on the team. I'm not sure how I knew this … maybe it was because I had parents and siblings who reinforced these concepts throughout my life, or some good coaches along the way that helped me internalize these views.

Mary Fry

We (the five authors of this book) have similar stories. We grew up with sport being a huge part of our lives. We spent many hours in our sports, interacting with a variety of coaches and teammates, and learning and developing on so many fronts because of our sport involvement. Arguably, many of our most meaningful childhood and adolescent experiences were associated with our sport experiences. We played sport through high school and college, and we used our sport experience to coach a variety of athletes. For each of us, having exposure to coaches who created a positive environment where effort, improvement, and caring were pervasive, left their lasting imprints on us.

At some point after our college experience, each of us decided to return to school (go to graduate school!) and take the opportunity to learn more about optimizing athletes' motivation in sport. Early on, each of us read work by John Nicholls and Joan Duda, two researchers who were addressing these very issues. We were hooked from that moment, and we have spent the last two plus decades learning, conducting research, and applying these concepts with a variety of athletes across different ages, levels (youth, high school, college sport), and skill levels. We have seen over and over again how the key to having great sport experiences is very much in the hands of coaches who know how to create the right environment for athletes. As co-authors, we have traveled very similar paths in our sport involvement, studies throughout graduate school, and our work as college faculty. We have written this book to share with others information about how to be part of this movement to create a caring and task-involving climate that results in positive sport experiences for all athletes. Though some coaches may be more interested in the material (Chapters 3–13) directly related to practice, we want to provide some information up-front in this book about the theory and research upon which all our recommendations are based.

Introduction to Nicholls' Motivation Theory Applied to Sport

Though multiple researchers were involved in developing theory and conducting research early on that laid the foundation for our work, John Nicholls played the biggest role.[1] Beginning in the late 1970s and continuing until his death in 1994, he was doing the groundwork for understanding the motivational processes that were key for helping individuals maximize their potential. Basically, he developed a comprehensive theory that outlined three fundamental components of motivation (See Table 1.1). For the sake of brevity, we are providing a brief overview of Nicholls' theory to give our readers some background for how this work has evolved.

Young Athletes' Understanding of Sport Ability

The first component of Nicholls' theory details how children's cognitive development occurs over the elementary school years. He described how very young children are incapable of understanding the concept of ability. They believe that high effort is synonymous with high ability (i.e., Whoever tries the hardest will perform the best), and they do not distinguish these concepts until they reach the upper elementary school grades. They also are incapable of distinguishing various levels of task difficulty. That is, adolescents and adults understand that if a small portion of athletes are able to do a task (hit a jump serve), it signifies high ability. Young children, instead, lack the mental capacity to recognize these distinctions. Instead, in their minds, all who try hard have high ability and will perform well. Worth noting is that children do not display a mature understanding of luck until they are approaching adolescence. Across the elementary years they are still believing that individuals have some control over performing well in luck tasks (e.g., "*If I try hard I can do well in my Candy Land game*" [a popular children's game based on luck]). Nicholls' research in this area, helped show how adults have a much stronger understanding of the concept of ability than do children.

One of the reasons Nicholls' work in this area was so significant is that he was able to show that children's delayed cognitive grasp of the concept of ability, serves as a protective factor to help them stay highly motivated through the elementary years. In fact, it is typically not until the middle and high school years that youngsters lose interest in school and other activities. Young children believe that high effort leads to positive outcomes and they do not yet accurately judge their ability in comparison to others, so there is no reason to withdraw effort.

TABLE 1.1 Key Elements in Nicholls' Motivation Theory

Nicholl's Motivation Theory Applied to Sport
• Children's Understanding of Sport Ability
• Athletes' Personal Definitions of Success (Goal Orientations)
• Athletes' Perceptions of Their Team Environment

Athletes' Development of Their Personal Definitions of Success

Eventually, though, all young people achieve this mature understanding of ability (around the age of 12 years), which leads to the second component of Nicholls's theory: Personal Definitions of Success. Nicholls outlined how the next step involves children developing their goal orientations or personal definitions of success. There are two goal orientations and all individuals have some level of both. When individuals have a high task orientation they define success based on their personal effort, improvement, and cooperation with others. They feel most successful in sport when they know they gave their best effort and are seeing improvement in their sport skills and knowledge of the game. Nicholls explained that a task orientation is preferred because the focus is on controllable factors. Everyone can try hard and improve with time. Another advantage is that everyone with a high task orientation can feel successful and they are more likely to sustain their motivation over time. Their satisfaction comes from knowing they are doing all they can to be the best that they can be. If the world was full of people who adopted a high task orientation, it would be transformational, because there would be a huge band of individuals who were coming closer to reaching both their sport and human potential.

The other personal definition of success is an ego orientation. Individuals with a high ego orientation define success based on how their performance compares to others. That is, they only feel successful if they win and/or outperform others. Their satisfaction comes from knowing that they are better than others. With this orientation, a limited number of athletes can feel successful. Nicholls and a host of researchers in sport psychology have painted a clear picture that athletes benefit from adopting a high task orientation and deemphasizing ego orientation. When individuals report high task orientation they reap many, many benefits, whereas a high ego orientation can be problematic, particularly for athletes who do not fair so well on the performance end. When a high ego orientation takes over for individuals, they can become discouraged easily if the outcome is not what they were targeting. In addition, if only those who have the best performances (and win) receive recognition and encouragement, the message becomes clear that those with less ability and/or current skill should direct their time and attention to other pursuits (quit sport for other activities). In some cases, this can lead to unfulfilled potential. Maybe these individuals would have soared if they had been encouraged to focus on their effort and improvement and been helped to see that their long-term development takes time. Even if athletes stick with sport, if they have a high ego orientation (combined with a low task orientation), they are not nearly as likely to have a fun and rewarding experience.

Other important points to make about goal orientations are that they can be considered the lenses through which individuals view the world and find purpose and meaning. They are somewhat general in that if individuals are task-oriented in one area of life (sport) it often crosses over to other areas of life (school), although not always. Also, if athletes are high in task or ego orientation, they are more likely to see an environment (or climate) they are in as reflecting that orientation. The last point about goal orientations is that everyone is to some degree both task and ego-oriented. It is true that some athletes are high in one orientation and low in the other, some might be high in both, and a few might be low in both orientations. Researchers have suggested that athletes who compete at higher levels of sport may be more likely to be high in both task and ego orientation. Research has revealed that it might not be harmful for athletes to be high in ego orientation as long as they have a high task orientation, but the bottom line is that to become motivated to learn a sport and then to sustain that motivation over time, a high task orientation is key.

The Climate on Sport Teams

This brings us to the third component of Nicholls' theory, the motivational climate. The motivational climate refers to the atmosphere that is created primarily by coaches but can also be impacted by everyone else in the sport including athletes, parents, officials, administrators, and fans. In creating a climate, coaches are emphasizing the important factors on the team (for example, winning vs. effort). Nicholls highlighted how individuals not only can define success based on the task and ego orientation lens but they can also view the climates in that way, seeing their team environment as encouraging athletes to focus on more task- than ego-involving aspects of sport. He described the features of a task-involving climate in contrast to an ego-involving climate. When coaches create a task-involving climate, they emphasize to athletes that effort and improvement are the qualities most highly valued and rewarded on the team, mistakes are embraced as part of the learning process, every athlete is made to feel that they play an important role on the team, and cooperation among teammates is fostered.

The Addition of Caring to the Sport Climate

The features identified by researchers (Nicholls, Ames, Duda) are critical to creating an optimal climate, and when done well by coaches, the benefits to athletes are obvious (see Chapter 2).[2, 3]

However, we began to conclude that an additional feature of the climate was necessary to add: a caring dimension. We determined that coaches also needed to focus on the relationships that develop among and between coaches and athletes. Maria Newton introduced our group to the work of Nel Noddings, an educational philosopher who has written extensively about the importance of teaching young people how to be in caring relationships.[4]

Noddings describes three conditions that are part of caring relationships. First, coaches must genuinely listen to their athletes. Sometimes, coaches can find themselves busy with all the responsibilities of coaching, and not be intentional in listening, hearing, and checking to be sure they really understand their athletes' thoughts and feelings. Noddings describes this as the first key to caring. The second key involves coaches using this information to support their team as both individuals and athletes in this world. Coaches who care want to support their athletes in setting and reaching goals, help them through disappointments, discuss their concerns, and help them see the potential they have to make both their community and the world a better place. Noddings explains that the last aspect of caring is recognizing that in coach–athlete relationships, the athletes have to recognize that the coach cares. In other words, for caring to occur, athletes must perceive it.

CLIMATE IN ACTION 1.1

My high school track coach, Warren Watson, was rather a tough minded guy, and it was sometimes hard to tell if he was just coaching us as a side job to his football coaching, but at the end of my first season he began to help me understand that running track could take me places beyond my current little world. I began to understand he was trying to genuinely help me as a person, to work at my sport to help me grow as a young man and as future professional, for whatever path in life I chose. I knew he cared about me and not just my 800 times. He also helped me understand that my father was right about so many of the same things. I remember many things Coach Watson told me, but I mostly remember how he made me feel – that I could be the one making choices for my life and how I wanted it to be.

Shared by DL Phillips

Noddings recognizes that it may be down the road before some athletes look back and realize how much their coach cared about them, and that is okay. Athletes sometimes recognize more and more the impact of their coach's caring as they continue down the road of life. The Climate in Action 1.1 quote by Darrell Phillips is a good example of this. Darrell describes a caring high school track coach who helped him see that he was in the driver's seat in life, and that he could choose to pursue ambitious goals. This coach did way more than help Darrell become a better athlete. He helped him see the bigger picture of his life. It is powerful to see Darrell reflecting back decades later, and remembering so clearly the difference his coach made in his life. Darrell went on to teach and coach many athletes, to obtain a PhD in sport psychology, and to be a difference maker, and his high school coach played an important role in all of it.

CLIMATE IN ACTION 1.2

Charlie [Coach Mazzone] was like a father figure for me. We had a deep emotional connection that went way beyond sport. To be honest, he didn't teach us a lot about our sport (because we were highly skilled), but the respect and admiration we had for him went beyond words. I had a crappy family life, so for me, this relationship with my coach may have been even more important than for my teammates. I just know that Charlie kept caring about me through my life after my college days ended, and there is no doubt about what a difference that has made for me as I matured into adulthood.

Shared by Rob Pearse

Rob Pearse, in Climate in Action 1.2, also describes a coach who had a lasting impact. Rob's family life was challenging and Coach Charlie Mazzone, beloved by dozens of athletes who played for him at the University of Memphis, provided love and support that was sorely needed in Rob's life. Rob notes how he and his coach had a deep connection that went beyond the competitions that occurred on a handball court. Charlie passed away in 2018, but the impact he had on those athletes who played for him continues.

Noddings believes so strongly in the power of caring that she has called for caring to be a primary goal of schools, to focus on helping youngsters both express and receive caring responses from others. After much discussion and reflection, we agreed with Noddings, and began to look at the value of coaches creating a caring climate for athletes. We describe a caring climate as occurring when athletes perceive their sport environment as "interpersonally inviting, safe, supportive, and able to provide the experience of feeling valued and respected."[5] On a deeper level, when athletes experience a caring climate in sport they perceive that they can be themselves, without risk of being teased or embarrassed. They sense that others genuinely care about them and have concern for what is going on in their lives, outside of sport. Athletes in a caring climate also feel a responsibility and recognize that they play a role in creating this climate. It requires every member of the team to be on board the caring bus, to see the part they play in expressing care for coaches and teammates.

Overall, there are five features that represent a caring and task-involving climate. These features, shown in Figure 1.1, represent the core of what coaches can do to establish an environment where all their athletes can thrive. An important point is that while athletes can have both a high task and ego orientation, when it comes to the climate, coaches cannot create both. They have to commit to creating either a caring and task-involving climate or an ego-involving climate. The reason is that the features of each of these climates are in direct contrast with one another. A coach cannot tell her athletes that effort and improvement are the most valued commodities on the team, but then constantly talk about winning. In a similar vein, a coach cannot teach athletes that mistakes are part of learning and then constantly punish mistakes, or indicate cooperation among athletes is the key, but then only foster rivalry. Clearly, a coach has to buy in and commit to creating one climate or the other. If a coach does not commit to either climate or tries to do both, the result is a neutral environment where the coaches' potential to have a positive impact is diminished. Additionally, we believe that a task-involving climate is further augmented when it is combined with a caring climate. Research, as will be described in more detail in the next chapter, has revealed that athletes who are fortunate enough to have coaches who create this climate are most likely to maximize both their athletic and human potential.

Our experience is that we see too few caring and task-involving climates in sport and too many ego-involving climates (Table 1.2). In an ego climate, coaches emphasize ability and performance rather than effort and improvement. They go to considerable lengths talking about the best athletes and those with the strongest performances, because they see that as motivating to all athletes (makes everyone want to be one of the athletes that gets hyped). Coaches are keyed in on the importance of winning and outperforming others. They also have the perspective that mistakes are bad and need to be punished. How else can athletes receive the message that mistakes are not what the team needs? Their view is that mistakes are not okay, and they typically have less interest in understanding why mistakes are made, and trust that athletes can figure it out themselves. In an ego-involving climate, coaches give most of their attention to the few stars on the team. They realize the stars are clutch to the team in terms of performance and they do not see

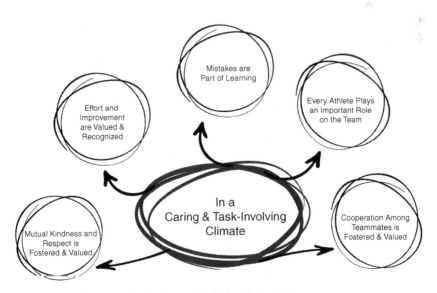

FIGURE 1.1 Features of a Caring and Task-Involving Climate

TABLE 1.2 Features of an Ego-Involving Climate

Features of an Ego-Involving Climate
• Ability and Performance Outcome are Most Highly Valued and Rewarded
• Mistakes are Punished
• A Few Star Players Receive Most of the Attention
• Rivalry Among Teammates is Encouraged

a conflict in favoring those athletes, since, from their perspective, they are contributing more to the team. Finally, in an ego-involving climate, coaches are creating rivalry among players on their team. They see this as a necessary aim in motivating their athletes. They want athletes to outperform each other and see each other as adversaries, as they feel that in the end it is beneficial to the team.

Researchers have painted a strong picture that an ego-involving climate is a rough place to spend time, and does not set athletes up to be their best. In fact, ego-involving climates create many casualties along the way including athletes whose confidence and interest in sport nosedived. A caring and task-involving climate, however, helps every athlete on the team be more likely to invest and strive to be the best they can be.

In this book, we lay out more specifically the reasons why creating a caring and task-involving climate should be the goal of every youth sport coach (and likely any coach [at any level] who is trying to optimize athletes' sport performances and experiences). In Chapter 2 we briefly summarize the 100s of research studies that have helped us arrive at the conclusion that all young athletes need a caring and task-involving climate. In Chapters 3–7, we describe each feature of a caring and task-involving climate, and provide many strategies coaches can use to help emphasize the particular features. In Chapters 8–10, we help coaches who have the goal of creating a caring and task-involving climate think about how to get the season started on the right foot, how to help particular groups of young athletes who may expressly benefit from being in a positive climate, and how to overcome challenges that coaches may experience in trying to establish the climate. Chapters 11–12 focus on two other parties that play a huge role in coaches' success with creating a caring and task-involving climate: parents and sport administrators. Finally, we bring it all together in Chapter 13.

We started this chapter by sharing how we all came to develop an interest in sport motivation. Our interest in motivation culminated as it led each of us to study at Purdue University, under the direction of Dr. Joan Duda, our mentor, who is a leader in the area of sport motivation. We all crossed paths there, and our friendships developed as graduate school peers. Some of us were at the end of our study when others were arriving, but our relationships all began in West Lafayette, Indiana in the 1990s.

Our story continued, though, as we graduated and began our careers as college faculty. We found ourselves at a variety of colleges/universities around the country where we were all continuing our efforts to study and to apply this theory to help coaches and athletes. We would meet up at conferences and share our experiences, and in the early 2000s, we decided to gather to have our own mini-motivation conference. Our first meeting was in Memphis, TN and that few days set us off on a collaborative journey that has been rich and rewarding for each of us. We began meeting each year and have continued this tradition for nearly 20 years. We have engaged in research together, but most important has been our continued support of one another both professionally and personally. We have helped one another through both our academic (e.g., sharing teaching activities, advice for advancing our careers) and personal lives (e.g., raising children, losing parents and pets, illness, a house fire), all the way providing a constant source of encouragement, interest in each other's lives, and caring. As we wrote this book, we marveled at how rare it is for a research group to stick together for so many years, and it struck us that the key was our ability to create a caring and task-involving climate within our group. In formulating our belief that creating this climate is key for sport teams, it has not escaped us that a caring and task-involving climate is crucial for all important aspects of life.

Thank you for your interest in learning more about the importance of creating a caring and task-involving climate in sport, and thank you for sharing our passion for making sport all it can be for young people. Let's encourage everyone to create an environment where we can work hard and be kind.

Reflecting on Practice

How Do the Ideas in this Chapter Align with your Approach to Coaching and to Life?

We provide a lot of information in this chapter and it is great for coaches to take time to reflect on what they think about the concepts. The questions below can provide a format for coaches to think about these concepts, and discuss them with others (assistant coaches, friends, athletes).

Self-Reflection

Definitions of Success

- How do I define success in sport? Do I want my athletes to feel successful when they give their best effort and improve or when they outperform or do better than others?
- How do I encourage my athletes to define success in sport?
- What kinds of things do I do or say that send the message about what success means for them as athletes and as an overall team?
- If my athletes were asked to describe how I define success in sport, what would they say?
- Do I buy in to the ideas presented in this chapter, that all athletes need a high task orientation?

Creating a Caring and Task-Involving Climate

- Am I intentional about creating a caring and task-involving climate? Or do I just hope it happens because this is my intention?
- What kinds of things do I say or do to send the message to my athletes that I want to have a caring and task-involving climate on the team? (Maybe I can ask others about this, watch a video of me coaching, etc.)
- Would some athletes see the climate on a team as more caring than other athletes? If so, what contributes to those differences?
- What would I define as my current strengths in creating a caring and task-involving climate? What features of the climate am I able to emphasize well with my athletes?
- What are my weaker areas for creating a caring and task-involving climate? Why might these be harder areas for me?
- Are there features of an ego-involving climate that are challenging for me to avoid promoting? Why might that be?

- What kinds of things might help me strengthen my ability to create a more caring and task-involving climate for my athletes?

Reflecting on these questions and discussing them with others (coaches, athletes, parents, administrators) can help coaches gain some sense of how they're doing and how they could have a greater positive impact on their athletes.

Sources

1   Nicholls, J. G. (1989). *The competitive ethos and democratic education.* Cambridge, MA: Harvard University Press.

2   Ames, C. (1992). Classrooms: Goals, structures, and student motivation. *Journal of Educational Psychology, 84,* 261–271.

3   Duda, J. L. (1998). *Advances in sport and exercise psychology measurement.* Champaign, IL: Human Kinetics.

4   Newton, M., Fry, M., Watson, D., Gano-Overway, L., Kim, M., Magyar, M., & Guivernau, M. (2007). Psychometric properties of the caring climate scale in a physical activity setting. *Revista de Psicologia del Deporte, 16,* 67–84.

5   Noddings, N. (1992). *The challenge to care in schools: An alternative approach to education.* New York, NY: Teachers College Press, [p. 70].

2

THE MANY BENEFITS OF CREATING A CARING AND TASK-INVOLVING CLIMATE IN SPORT

Highlights

- When coaches create a caring and task-involving climate, they set the stage for their athletes to have a positive sport experience and improved performance.
- When coaches create a caring and task-involving climate there are also opportunities that extend to life outside of sport as athletes have opportunities to develop life skills and boost their mental and physical health.

In the previous chapter, we outlined the defining characteristics of a caring and task-involving climate. However, coaches may still wonder why it is important to implement this type of climate in practice. The answer is that a caring and task-involving climate is a winning combination. It benefits motivation and performance and it creates a positive atmosphere where athletes and coaches want to belong. It also benefits athletes' life outside of sport. Here is a short review of what researchers have found (See Sources at the end of the chapter to learn more about research in this area).

Benefits within the Sport Experience

As noted in the last chapter, a task-involving climate focuses on recognizing the importance of effort and striving to improve. Thus, it may not be surprising that when athletes perceive a task-involving climate they want to apply effort and use strategies to get better. Specifically, when athletes perceive that their coaches focus on helping them improve and learn from their mistakes, they state they try harder at tasks and use strategies to improve their athletic practices like set goals, use feedback from coaches, and maintain focus. In contrast, when a coach creates an ego-involving climate, shown by an emphasis on outdoing others, developing team rivalries, and punishing mistakes, athletes report less effort and fewer strategies to improve practice. This is lamentable since applying effort and using effective strategies are key for improving performance and encouraging athletes to exert control over their own athletic development.

A caring and task-involving climate is also connected to positive experiences in sport. For example, athletes in a caring and task-involving climate report having enjoyable and fun sport experiences. In contrast, athletes in an ego-involving climate say they experience more anxiety and less enjoyment. In the end, who wants to be in an environment that is anxiety provoking and not fun. Additionally, having more anxiety can negatively affect athletic performance as anxious feelings can disrupt athletes' focus during competitions and interfere with their movement patterns. Therefore, enhancing enjoyment and decreasing anxiety can have positive outcomes for both motivation and performance.

Another aspect of the sport experience enhanced in a caring and task-involving climate is good sport conduct. Athletes who perceive the climate to be more cooperative, respectful, and kind with an emphasis on improving one's performance against a worthy opponent also report engaging in respectful behavior toward opponents and officials, having greater respect for the rules of the sport, and helping others. In many ways, it appears that a caring and task-involving climate creates an environment that supports the spirit of the game. On the other hand, an ego-involving climate is not related to helping behaviors and, at times, has been associated with disrespectful behavior and poor sport conduct.

Improved relations among team members is another positive benefit of a caring and task-involving climate. Athletes like their teammates and coaches more and report higher levels of team chemistry as the climate becomes more caring and task-involving. Further, a task-involving climate is related to better athlete-coach relationships and a caring climate is related to engaging in more caring behaviors toward teammates. It seems that a focus on respect and kindness where all members are valued and team members work together and help one another improve creates a sense of community among members of the team.

In the end, it may not be surprising that caring and task-involving climates are associated with a greater overall commitment from the athlete while an ego-involving climate is not. When athletes have the opportunity to make personal improvements through their own effort, feel a sense of enjoyment and low levels of anxiety, and like their team members, it makes sense that they would want to be part of the team. In fact, athletes, who perceive these climates, are less likely to drop out of their sport and are more likely to commit to coming back the next season (see Figure 2.1).

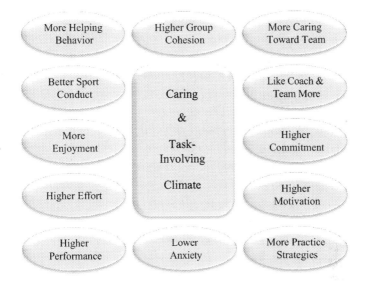

FIGURE 2.1 Benefits within the Sport Experience

Benefits for Health and Life

Youth sport coaches recognize that their goal is not only to help their athletes improve their athletic performance and develop within a team but also to help them become better people. Fortunately, a caring and task-involving climate positively relates to important life skills and mental and physical health (see Figure 2.1).

In looking at life skills, when athletes perceive a more caring and task-involving climate they report being more empathetic toward others, helping another person in need, being nice to another, taking initiative in completing tasks, and using more social skills.

Benefits to mental health also exist. As perceptions of the caring climate increase, athletes report lower levels of depression and sadness and higher levels of happiness and hopefulness. In addition, they indicate greater confidence in their ability to control both their positive and negative emotions. A task-involving climate has also been positively related with self-esteem. These outcomes suggest that coaches developing this type of climate may help athletes improve their mental well-being.

Improvements in physical health have been shown to connect to the climate as well. When individuals are placed in a caring and task-involving climate, they have a lower stress response (that is, less cortisol) compared to those placed in a more ego-involving climate. Additionally, when athletes perceive a caring and task-involving climate they are more likely to report concussion symptoms, which is critical for their physical recovery.

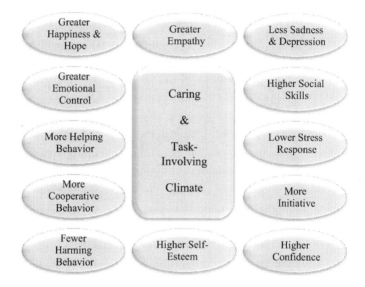

FIGURE 2.2 Benefits for Health and Life

*****

As described in this chapter, coaches provide a better athlete experience when they develop a caring and task-involving climate on their sport teams. Creating a caring and task-involving climate sets the stage for personal success in sport and life. When coaches focus on developing athletes' techniques and tactics to help them improve, invest their own time in helping all of their athletes strive for excellence, set high expectations linked to effort and improvement, get to know all of their athletes, create opportunities to meet their needs, encourage athletes to learn from their mistakes, and teach athletes the importance of supporting, valuing, and respecting one another's success on and off the field, positive results abound. These positive results are not only specific to physical development within sport, but also provide opportunities for coaches to facilitate development of life skills and maintain positive mental and physical health. In the end, this success is not only satisfying for athletes but also parents and coaches. The next section of the book will highlight five key features and possible strategies for building a caring and task-involving climate within the sport environment so coaches can maximize the athletes' sport experience.

Reflecting on Practice

Part of excellent coaching is reflecting on coaching practice and how it might be improved. If this chapter has you pondering, "I wonder what influence I am having on my athletes?", it may be useful to conduct some informal evaluations. Here are a few activities you can use to find out.

Self-Reflection

Review the benefits of creating a caring and task-involving climate below. Check those benefits that you value and hope you foster among athletes on your team.

☐	Trying hard	☐	Having strong team chemistry on the team
☐	Being motivated	☐	Liking their coach and team
☐	Using good practice strategies (like setting goals, maintaining focus)	☐	Being helpful and kind
☐	Showing more initiative	☐	Being caring toward others
☐	Committing to the sport	☐	Being empathetic and considering another person's perspective
☐	Enjoying their sport participation	☐	Being happy and hopeful
☐	Being less stressed	☐	Being more confident
☐	Engaging in good sport conduct	☐	Having good social skills

- Which of the benefits checked do I feel like my athletes are experiencing right now on my team?
- What things do I see in my athletes that make me think they are experiencing these benefits?
- What benefits am I not seeing right now but would love to see in my athletes?

Observing Your Athletes

- Observe your athletes and consider the following:
  - ☐ What does their effort look like in practice?
  - ☐ Do you see athletes making improvements in their skills?
  - ☐ Are they focusing on ways to improve their performance during practice?
  - ☐ Are they performing well in competitions?
  - ☐ Are they smiling during practice?
  - ☐ Are they psyched to put in the time and effort outside of practice to get better?
  - ☐ Do they appear confident?
  - ☐ Are they supporting each other in practice and competition?
  - ☐ Are teammates nice to one another?
  - ☐ Are athletes working together in practice and competitions?
  - ☐ Do some athletes get left out or are there cliques?
  - ☐ Do they exhibit good sport conduct during competitions?
  - ☐ Are they respectful to teammates, family, opponents, and officials?
  - ☐ Do athletes stay with the program and participate year after year?

- What did you learn?

If your observations indicate that your athletes have many positive benefits outlined in this chapter (for example, they give effort, support one another in practice, engage in good sport conduct) you may be successfully implementing a caring and task-involving climate.

Conversations with Trusted Athletes

Talk with some of your athletes to get a sense of how they think the season is going. Doing so can help you determine whether your observations are similar to the perceptions of your athletes. Below are some questions to consider. If you feel that you may get more honest responses using anonymous surveys with all the athletes on your team, use the questions below to create a survey for your athletes to complete during the season.

- ☐ Are you enjoying the season so far?
- ☐ What would you identify as the main values on our team?
- ☐ Can you tell me about the improvements that you have made this season? Are there ways I can continue to help the team improve?
- ☐ What have you observed about team effort? Are people trying hard and focused during practice? What ways have you seen me reinforce this effort?
- ☐ Have you felt supported by me and your teammates during practices and competitions?
- ☐ Do you feel our team is respectful to others on the team?
- ☐ Do you feel like you are a valued member of the team? Do you feel like all members of the team feel like they are valued and important contributors to the team?
- ☐ Do you feel like team members help one another during practice?
- ☐ Do you feel like we are working together well as a team?

- What did you learn?

If your conversation or survey responses indicate that your athletes have many positive benefits outlined in this chapter (for example, they give effort, support one another in practice, engage in good sport conduct) you may be successfully implementing a caring and task-involving climate.

Sources

Fry, M. D., & Hogue, C. M. (2018). Psychological considerations for children in sport and performance. In O. Braddick (Ed.), *Oxford Research Encyclopedia of Psychology*. New York: Oxford University Press.

Fry, M. D., & Moore, E. W. (2019). Motivation in sport: Theory and application. In M. H. Anshel (Ed.), T. Petrie, E. Labbe, S. Petruzzello, & J. Steinfeldt (Assoc. Eds.), *APA handbook of sport and exercise psychology: Vol. 1. Sport psychology*. Washington, DC: American Psychological Association.

Harwood, C., Keegan, R. J., Smith, J. M. J., & Raine, A. S. (2015). A systematic review of the intrapersonal correlates of motivational climate perceptions in sport and physical activity. *Psychology of Sport and Exercise, 18*, 9–25.

PART II

Features of a Caring and Task-Involving Climate in Sport

3

FEATURES OF A CARING AND TASK-INVOLVING CLIMATE IN SPORT

Mutual Kindness and Respect is Fostered and Valued

Highlights

- By making connections with all athletes coaches foster mutual kindness and respect.
- Athletes see the value of mutual kindness and respect when coaches intentionally communicate these values to their team.
- Mutual kindness and respect is fostered when coaches act with care to support each athlete on the team.

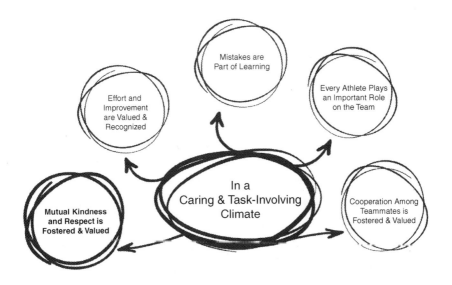

One of the integral features of a caring and task-involving climate in sport is creating a spirit of mutual kindness and respect within the team. While this may seem like an easy task (i.e., people just need to be respectful and kind), creating this type of atmosphere requires intentionality. Coaches need to be purposeful in developing trusting relationships with team members and letting them know they are valued and appreciated. This happens by establishing a community where values such as kindness, respect, generosity, and care are front and center and are visibly acted upon within the team by both the coach and athletes. Therefore, this chapter focuses on specific ideas for coaches to be intentional in developing mutual kindness and respect by making connections, communicating with care, and acting with care.

Make Connections

Critical to treating others with kindness and respect is understanding who they are as people. Therefore, taking a genuine interest in athletes and getting to know them not only sets the tone that everyone matters, but also helps coaches know how to act with kindness and respect toward each athlete. Many coaches do this regularly, however here are a few suggestions that may help coaches connect with athletes and help athletes connect with one another.

Welcome Athletes Daily to Practice

Greeting each athlete sets the tone that coaches are happy to see them. For example, "*Hi Olivia, glad to have you here today!*". Coaches can do a collective greeting and fill them in on the activities for the day and take questions. For instance, "*Welcome back, everyone! Our focus for today will be on aerobic work – so long and strong sets to build our endurance to go long distances. Any questions before we get started?*". Coaches can also create a habit of having athletes greet one another like, "*Okay, before we start our first set, high-five everyone in your lane.*"

Get to Know All Athletes

An enjoyable aspect of coaching is getting to know the athletes and sharing the ups and downs in their lives. Yet, in the midst of the time consuming and task driven life of a coach, coaches can sometimes forget to embrace the importance of building relationships with their athletes. Here are a few strategies to remind coaches to get to know all of their athletes:

- A good first step is learning the name of every athlete on the team. While this seems straightforward, some athletes report that their coach did not know their name for weeks or months into the season.

- Another important step earlier in the season is getting to know the new members of the team. It can be extremely stressful for athletes when they join a new team. A big concern is whether they will fit in and be accepted on the team. It makes a big difference for athletes when coaches go out of their way to get to know them and welcome them to the team. Additionally, coaches can address concerns they have with making the transition which can further help to reduce their stress.

- Coach can also learn athletes' interests, joys, strengths, and weaknesses as it relates to their sport. Understanding each athlete can help with practice planning. For example, a high school volleyball coach discussed how she had her athletes complete a worksheet at the beginning of each season identifying their interests (e.g., favorite color, birthdate, drills they like to do and ones they do not). She used the information during the season. First, as she prepared practice, she chose those drills players like to do. If she could, she avoided those drills that players did not like to do. If she had to use them, she at least told them why the drill was important and tried to make it enjoyable. Through this act, she let them know that she cared enough to include their interests. Second, she also would bring in cupcakes with icing in their favorite color for their birthday. These and other little acts of kindness made the athletes feel appreciated.

- Really getting to know athletes means learning about their life outside of sport. Don Hellison,[1] in *Teaching personal and social responsibility through physical activity*, suggests engaging in brief relational encounters by greeting athletes, asking them questions about their day, and listening to their thoughts and opinions. This allows athletes to share as little or as much as they would like about their day and about their life outside of sport. For example, during warm-ups in lacrosse, the coach may walk up and down the field as athletes are doing dynamic stretches and check in with athletes (e.g., *"Hey Sarah, how did your school day go? How are you feeling about the upcoming choir concert?"*). In another instance, a coach might use recovery days to check in with swimmers. That is, while the team is swimming a long recovery set the coach can set up one lane to work on technique. Then the coach calls a swimmer over to the lane to work on a stroke but at the same time checks in. During the practice, the coach could make connections with four or five swimmers.

Use the Power of Observation

Watching athletes in practice and games can also help coaches get to know athletes. Sir Alex Ferguson talks about his use of observation as key to his success as a coach for Manchester United football:[2]

> *What you can pick up by watching is incredibly valuable... Seeing a change in a player's habits or a sudden dip in his enthusiasm allowed me to go further with*

him: Is it family problems? Is he struggling financially? Is he tired? What kind of mood is he in? Sometimes I could even tell that a player was injured when he thought he was fine. I don't think many people fully understand the value of observing. I came to see observation as a critical part of my management skills. The ability to see things is key — or, more specifically, the ability to see things you don't expect to see.

In this quote, we see how Coach Ferguson uses his observational skills to start a conversation with the intent of finding out what might be happening with a player. He is seeking to understand his athletes, rather than assuming they do not care or are not motivated. This starting point helps him provide a better experience for the athletes and helps them better reach their potential. The key message to athletes is that they matter and the coach wants to help them. Additionally, by seeking to understand athletes through observation, coaches are challenged to see the unexpected and to take our blinders off to see beyond the Xs and Os.

CLIMATE IN ACTION 3.1

I think it is really important to develop your observational skills to know what may be going on with an athlete. For example, I noticed an athlete wearing a wristband which she had never worn before during practice. I pulled her aside and asked her about the wristband. I discover that she had been cutting herself. In conversation with her and her parents, we assisted her in getting the help she needed. However, if I had not taken the time to notice I may have not been able to help.

Shared by Coach Reggie Blackmon

Structure Opportunities for Team Members to Get to Know One Another

Creating an environment that promotes mutual kindness and respect cannot stop with just the coach making connections with athletes. Athletes also need to be encouraged to make connections with each other to build trust, understanding, and friendships, all of which set the stage for mutual kindness and respect. Coaches can provide structured and intentional opportunities in practices, on the way to games, and outside of athletics for athletes to get to know one another. Here are some intentional activities designed to help teammates get to know one another:

- During preseason, coaches can pair new and old players and have them conduct teammate interviews. Coaches can give them a series of questions, both general and fun, they can ask one another and then have them introduce their partner to the group.

- Ask veteran players to make an effort to say hello to new members of the team at the start of each practice.
- During warm-ups, ask athletes to complete this sentence either in front of the whole team or in small groups:
  o   I love soccer because …
  o   My favorite athlete is …
  o   The thing I like about school is …
  o   One thing I like to do on the weekend is …
- Swim Coach Lanny Landtroop[3] suggests having athletes write the name of a tangible item (e.g., Mount Rushmore) on a sticky note and then collects them all. The coach then randomly hands out the sticky notes to athletes, who stick them on their forehead. They then walk around introducing themselves to each member of the team and asking yes-no questions about the item written on their sticky note. The game continues until everyone has had a chance to meet and then individuals try to guess their item.
- Work with parent volunteers to plan outings for the team.
  o   Go to the lake for a day of swimming.
  o   Have a talent show or karaoke night so athletes can display their other talents.
  o   Create a scavenger hunt or geocaching event.
  o   Have the team go to another school sponsored event together as a team to support their classmates.
  o   Have the team create team t-shirts.
  o   Organize an adventure activity like a ropes course, zip lining, or whitewater rafting.

Coaches need to be aware that some athletes might feel out of their comfort zone when engaging in social activities. Therefore, having coaches who get to know them and create activities that respect their boundaries and patiently encourage them to engage with others can make all the difference.

Structure Opportunities to Get Know Athletes' Family Members

Mutual kindness and respect can also extend to an athlete's family. While we recognize that coaches want to help athletes learn to speak for themselves, there is value in getting to know families in the right place and at the right time. Family members want to be part of the athletes' sport experience and coaches can help them by modeling how to positively interact with others and how to create trusting and collaborative relationships. Additionally, coaches can learn so much more about an athlete by learning the family's customs and traditions which could help them create a more positive experience for the athlete as well as enrich the life of the coach and other members of the team. Many coaches speak with delight in building family relationships and keeping in touch with families over time, even after the athletes move on to the next level. Here are a few ideas for coaches to consider in getting to know families:

- Create opportunities to interact with families. For example, a high school swim coach asked each class, like the sophomore athletes and their families, to provide small snacks for the rest of the team and their families after each home swim meet. It was a great way to help the coach get to know families and for family members to share their favorite recipes with the team. Other activities that coaches could do include:
  - o Host a cookout at a local park and invite parents to play a pick-up soccer game with their son/daughter.
  - o Create a special section for athletes' family members to sit during a game. Place a small note on the bleacher for those who attend that thanks them for coming and how best to support their goals for the competition.
  - o After a team win, invite athletes and their family to the local pizza parlor to celebrate.
  - o Throughout the season, offer invitations to a small number of families to attend practice. They can see what occurs during practice and then post practice the coach can spend some time talking with the family members.
- Help family members know the boundaries for appropriate communication and interactions. For example, one local high school coach tells parents at the beginning of the year meeting that he wants to get to know them and wants to hear their concerns. Therefore, he will talk to parents about anything except their athletes' playing time. He will only talk to athletes about playing time. Another coach discussed how he told parents that if their athlete complains about practice, games, playing time, etc. to encourage the athlete to talk with the coach and then call him to discuss the concern out of earshot from the athlete. It helped to alleviate many misperceptions and helped the coach and parent work together to determine how best to move forward regarding the athlete's concern. It really helped to build trust between the coach and parents and helped parents feel part of the team.
- Invite family members to share their gifts with the team. By inviting family members to be part of the team it can help coaches get to know the athlete and their family. For example, a family may want to invite the team to their house for a pre-game dinner, provide a small motivational gift prior to the championship game, or share a family tradition. When this invitation is accepted it creates a positive environment where athletes and their families support one another. However, when there is no invitation or coaches react negatively it can be devastating.

CLIMATE IN ACTION 3.2

When I was in middle school, I was playing basketball and during the winter break my family made these special cookies that take a lot of time and effort. They are a big deal in my family and everyone acts like they are a huge deal when we have them. That year my mom wanted to share a plate of the cookies with my coach, and I told her that wasn't a good idea. I didn't think he would care about cookies, but my mom insisted that he would value and appreciate them. I will never forget when I carried that plate into the gym before practice, and said, "Hey Coach, my family made these cookies for you; they're kind of a big deal in my family." The coach looked at me like I was an idiot and like I was a 5-year-old, and after what seemed like 20 seconds he said, "Put them on the bleachers." I was humiliated, and told my mom later how he responded. I have never given a coach a cookie since that day and I'm sure I never will. That incident confirmed for me that I should always keep a distance with coaches and never get too personal.

Shared by an Anonymous Athlete

This incident is so insignificant in one way, but this coach missed out on recognizing how much the family cared for his efforts to work with young athletes. He also missed out on an opportunity to build a relationship with not only one of his athletes but also the athletes' family. The damage done in this small act of disrespect had a lasting impact. Had the coach shown appreciation for this gift, it would have gone a long way in creating a special bond with his athlete and the family.

Communicate Care

While developing positive and respectful relationships with athletes begins the process of developing a climate of mutual respect and kindness, learning to clearly communicate these values, verbally and nonverbally, is an important next step. On the surface, this entails explicitly communicating kindness and respect as team values but it also means that respect and kindness becomes a regular part of team communication and action. We offer the following ideas for communicating these values within sport programs.

Communicate Kindness and Respect as Part of Team Values

To emphasize mutual respect and kindness on teams, we need to set up ground rules of how the team operates (set the community norms). Therefore, a coach may include the following as team rules or communicate these team values:

- On this team, we treat each other with respect. That is, we are supportive of each other, we respectfully disagree, we avoid biases.
- On this team, we are kind, meaning we provide others encouraging words (no put downs), we listen without interrupting, and we engage in random acts of kindness (our team is a no bullying zone).

Throughout the season, coaches can highlight kindness and respect along with other team values in multiple ways. Here are a few examples:

- Tell stories of past team members or others that highlight the importance of respect, kindness, trust, patience, generosity, safety, acceptance, care, concern, etc.
  - o A coach recounts a time when Wendy and her family really demonstrated an act of kindness when she invited the whole team over to her house for a team picnic.
  - o A coach reminds the team how the previous year they organized a fundraiser and donation drive to help a local family who lost everything in a house fire.
  - o A coach shares when Nikki, an autistic child, was a member of the team and her teammates looked beyond her differences and saw the strengths she brought to the team. This is what full acceptance on this team is all about and what this team represents.
  - o A coach recalls when an athlete, who was a junior on the team, got injured and how the seniors supported her. They took turns going to rehabilitation sessions with the athlete. They also invited the athlete to attend practice sessions to be a team leader by leading warm ups, encouraging others and providing instructional feedback during practice, and providing encouraging words prior to games.
- Use positive and negative events within the community or larger sporting world as teachable moments to discuss team values. For example, when Roger Federer noticed many tennis players engaging in disrespectful behavior towards ball boys and ball girls he reminded players about the importance of being respectful and trying to control their emotions during tennis matches.[4] A tennis coach could share this example with the team and discuss the importance of respecting all those who help make the game possible.
- Have athletes share stories of when they have seen these values in action during the previous week or have them engage in "show and tell" of a role model who exhibits respect, kindness, or a helpful attitude.
  - o *"My friend, Tyrone, stood up to someone who was picking on me and telling me I couldn't do something because I was a girl. He reminded them that girls can do it. I really appreciated how he went out of his way to help me."*
  - o *"Michele saw me sitting by myself at lunch and came over to sit with me. Thanks for being kind."*

o   On Martin Luther King Jr. Day, Jenna shares with her team how she is inspired by Dr. King's work of fighting for inequality and reminding all of us the importance of treating everyone with respect. She notes her desire to be respectful to others and work toward finding common ground when she disagrees with others on the team.

- When coaches see athletes exhibit team values they should be sure to positively reinforce these behaviors either publicly or privately.

  o   *"Jake, thank you for saying hello to Marc* [the new member of the team] *and partnering up with him during our dribbling drills. You showed real kindness. Well done!"*

  o   High-Five Jeff after he goes over to talk to a teammate who seems a bit down and tries to cheer him up.

  o   *"Everyone, before we go today, I want to give a shoutout to Julia for helping her opponent up off the field. It showed real class. This is what respect is all about. Nice job."*

Communicate Acceptance and Value of All Team Members

Coaches can help everyone on the team feel a sense of belonging on the team. They can do this by letting athletes know they are part of the team, letting every member of the team know how they are integral to the team's success, and/ or sending a note to each athlete noting belief in their ability. Acceptance can be particularly difficult when athletes are paying attention to their differences rather than their similarities. An athlete who wears a hijab, has depression, wears out of style clothes, engages in different religious practices, use pronouns different than their sex, lacks social skills, has a physical disability, etc. can be perceived as "different" by other members of the team either consciously or unconsciously. This perceived difference may lead some athletes to not be as accepting of teammates. Coaches can encourage acceptance by helping athletes see how they are more similar than different. For example, playing a game of similar and different. This involves having youth stand in a line and ask questions like, *"Do you like ice cream? Do you like brussel sprouts? Do you speak a language other than English? Do you like superhero movies?"* and having them move left (yes) or right (no). Athletes can begin to see the many things they have in common. Coaches can also help team members by modeling inclusion and acceptance of all athletes. An example of this is shared by Michael and Cathy Hoffman.[5] They share the story of how their son Matthew, who has Down's syndrome, is included on his middle school soccer team. Throughout the season it is clear that the players follow the lead of their coach and accept Matthew as a member of the team and come to celebrate his successes. The beauty of creating an environment of mutual kindness and respect is that athletes understand that it is a safe place for them to be themselves, express their uncertainty, and know that they will be fully accepted.

Communicate Feedback in Constructive Ways

Sometimes when coaches are stressed, depressed, or frustrated, they do not consider the feelings of others when giving feedback. For example, an exasperated coach might say, "*How many times have I told you that for this play you pass it to the outside man? Are you even listening?*" Other coaches act to intimidate, demean, insult, or humiliate players in an effort to toughen up an athlete. For instance, coaches who yell at players out of frustration or call out athletes and make fun of them in front of others for a bad play are acting to intimidate and humiliate athletes. Some coaches focus on the worth of the player rather than the behavior (for example, "*What use are you to the team? I cannot believe I gave you a varsity spot on this team.*"). However, these behaviors undermine the credibility of the coach as they demonstrate the coach is inconsistent, moody, or not trustworthy. They also negatively impact athletes by creating anxiety that can interrupt effective decision making during games, reduce enjoyment, or undermine confidence. These actions also do not promote respect for individuals. Therefore, as coaches it is important to consider how to give feedback that is constructive, kind, and respectful. Here are a few examples:

- When a player comes out of a game after making several critical errors, a coach could say, "*AJ, I bet you're frustrated that it didn't go as planned. Just take a deep breath, it's alright. Let's run something that plays to your strengths and we will work on this other play in practice. I believe in you.*"
- When a player has disappointing times in both track events at a meet, a coach could say, "*Victoria, I know this is disappointing. What do you think happened?* (athlete responds) *How do you think we can improve that?* (athlete responds) *Okay, I have some ideas about how we might work on that. Let's plan to work on this in practice next week. I know we can make improvements.*"
- A swimmer continues to use incorrect stroke technique after being taught the correct form and being provided cues periodically over the course of several practices. Rather than becoming frustrated, the coach could act with respect and understanding. For example, the coach could video the swimmer and then ask the swimmer to watch the video and make comparisons to a swimmer using the correct form. The swimmer could be questioned about differences and what improvements she would need to make. The coach could provide positive feedback when she gives correct responses and offer her instructive feedback about how to make the improvements. The coach could then suggest they set up another video session to look at progress.
- Following a game where the players performed poorly, the coach could choose to discuss strengths and weaknesses following the game without losing self-control and then the next practice could be structured to help work on weaknesses in a non-punitive way. For example, a coach might say the next day in practice, "*I think we all recognize that our performance was not what we*

expect for ourselves. I have been reflecting on our areas of weakness during the game and I believe what I have planned for this practice will make us a stronger team").

Within the examples provided, coaches focus on treating the athlete with kindness and respect while also providing honest and informative feedback. As Bill Walsh recognized years ago on his NFL football teams,

> *insensitive, hammer-like shots that are delivered in the name of honesty and openness usually do the greatest damage to people. The damage ends up reverberating throughout the entire organization. Over time, people will lose the bonding factor they need for success. And over time, that directness will isolate you from the people with whom you work.*[6]

Therefore, we seek to be sensitive, respectful, and honest while still helping our athletes recognize their strengths and working to navigate or accept their weaknesses.

Listen and Respond with Empathy

We all recognize that people need to do a better job listening to one another and this can be extremely important in developing good coach–athlete relationships. While coaches are fairly familiar with active listening skills like maintaining good eye contact, not being distracted when someone is talking to them, seeking clarification, etc., coaches may be less familiar with understanding what are important things to attend to when talking with athletes. In attending to athletes, coaches want to get a sense of how athletes are feeling, what athletes are asking for and why, and what athletes need. Therefore, skills in empathy, understanding how it feels from their perspective and feeling what they feel, is very important. Coaches want to clarify feelings and thoughts from their athletes (for example, *"How does that make you feel?"* or *"Tell me what you're thinking?"*), acknowledge their feelings and thoughts (for example, *"I imagine that is really frustrating."*), avoid biases in seeking to understand their perspective (for example, athletes are not necessarily complaining just because they did not get playing time) and make athletes the center of the conversation (for example, saying to oneself it is not about me). For example, when a coach sits down to talk with an athlete who just learned of a season ending injury, it is important to listen, understand feelings, understand thoughts, and provide reassurance and support. Here are two sample responses:

- *"Jeremy, tell me what you learned from the doctor. (Listen and acknowledge feelings) Jeremy, it sounds like you are in a lot of pain and disappointed that this means that you cannot play the rest of the season. (Listen and acknowledge thoughts and provide reassurance and support). You do have a lot of things to consider right now related to preparing for surgery, keeping up with schoolwork, making it to rehabilitation appointments, and thinking about your role on the team. How can I help?"*

- *"Marlene, this is a lot to manage, how are you doing?* (Listen and acknowledge feelings). *How frustrating.* (Listen and acknowledge thoughts and provide reassurance and support). *"It sounds like you are concerned about not being part of the team. While we both know you cannot play, I can reassure you that you still are part of this team. We need your leadership and expertise."*

Lanny Landtroop[7] makes an insightful comment about communicating with athletes when he notes that communication with athletes revolves around the answer to three basic questions, "Do you care about me? Can you help me? Can I trust you?" Listening to our athletes' motives, needs, and feelings with empathy can help us communicate more effectively and demonstrate that we have their best interest in mind.

CLIMATE IN ACTION 3.3

As a collegiate field hockey coach, I have been working with the other coaching staff to encourage our athletes on and off the field. One way that I do this is by maintaining an open-door policy. I have established this and created a welcoming environment for any of my athletes that need to come talk to someone about field hockey, school, friend drama or anything else in their life that they need to get off their chest. Over this past year, I have really noticed a difference in my athletes. I now have girls running to my office to show me a test grade or just coming in to chat when they have 10 minutes before their next class. This atmosphere was always something that I wanted to implement into my coaching and provide for my athletes because I know that college can be stressful at times. My hope is to continue to be there for my athletes even if it is as simple as just listening to them.

Shared by Coach Marisa Sims

Provide Encouragement

A final idea for communicating care is for coaches to look for opportunities to provide encouragement. This can be simply using observational skills to know when an athlete might need an encouraging word during practice and games. For example, a coach might respond to an athlete, *"Lisa, you look tired. I know this running set is hard but it will help you get better. Keep it up."* Coaches can also encourage players to provide encouragement to one another. Here are a couple of ideas:

- Have athletes create their own positive statement that they then pass along to another team member before the end of practice.
- Have a High Five practice drill or set in which athletes High Five each other when a player has a successful attempt at a particular skill or tactic.

Act with Care

Carl Jung, a twentieth-century psychologist is credited with saying, "*You are what you do, not what you say you'll do.*"[8] Therefore, creating an environment of mutual respect and kindness means coaches need to also act this way toward others.

Model Kindness and Respect

Throughout this chapter there have been examples of how coaches can model kindness and respect by engaging in an act of kindness like celebrating everyone's birthday and accommodating athletes' interest in practice or being respectful like providing feedback in a constructive way and honoring someone who engaged in positive behavior. However, it is also important to point out that coaches are role models and when they act with compassion, dignity, respect, and kindness toward others their athletes learn how to interact with others. Therefore, how coaches treat officials, opponents, and community fans matters. It is important to remember that others are watching and if coaches fall short of reaching their team values they need to let the team know why and how they will work to improve it in the future.

Modeling respect and kindness requires coaches to also practice good self-control. When there is a bad call or the team loses a close game it is important to realize that all eyes are on the coach. Athletes look to their coaches to show them how to respond. Therefore, how coaches respond sets the stage for how their athletes will respond. It is important that coaches do not have a negative outburst. If they do then their athletes will internalize this as the 'right' way to react when things get a bit heated. In these heated moments, coaches should take a moment, just a second or two, to gather themselves and think about what behaviors would be best to model in this intense situation. Coaches might 'want' to yell or get after the referees or get on players. But it is better to show some restraint and con-sider what they 'should' do. Likely, after pausing a moment or two coaches realize that a calm, supportive, thoughtful response is the way to go. In doing so coaches respond in a respectful and kind tone and athletes will see that on their team this is how we behave and treat others.

The same level of self-control can apply to how coaches talk about athletes to other people. For example, after a frustrating loss a coach who speaks angrily about an athlete's poor performance to a group of fans after the game is being unkind and engaging in poor self-control. If the coach had taken a step back and reflected upon the athlete's overall performance and how the negative comments would impact the athlete (as the athlete is sure to hear the comments), the coach would have realized a different path was needed to model respect and maintain credibility in the eyes of the athlete.

Support Athletes

Coaches also act with care when they seek to support athletes in achieving their goals. Excellent coaches recognize that it is important to use the talent and skills of each player on their team to create a successful season. Therefore, supporting athletes in reaching their potential really supports team success and, more critically, sends the message that participating on this team is about them and not just about getting the win. Coaches, who act with care, go out of their way to help each athlete succeed. Here are a few examples:

- Coaches can meet with each athlete at the beginning of the year to identify season goals. With these goals in mind, create practices that will support their athletes' goals. During practices, discuss with athletes how the practice is supporting their goals. For instance, a coach responds, "*Today we are going to work on our dribbling skills. Jon, Paul, and Bill, I really created this practice to help you make progress toward your goals. Let's go out their and really work on meeting those goals.*"
- Coaches remind athletes the potential they see in them by creating challenges in practice and recognizing their excellent work when they achieve those challenges. For example, a coach might say to an athlete, "*Wow Robyn, look at the improvement you are making. I know these challenges are tough but they are definitely making you a better point guard. Thank you for taking on the challenge to improve your skills for yourself and the team.*"
- When an athlete is injured, coaches support their rehabilitation by checking in with how it is going and asking how they can help. Additionally, coaches demonstrate support when they invite the athlete to come to practice to stay connected and keep up to speed on adjustments in play. For example, a coach might tell her athlete, "*Hey Kristen, we are going to go over different ways to switch the attack. Why don't you come and watch. Even though you can't play you will learn a lot from watching that you can add to your imagery practice. It will really help you when you come back.*" Finally, supportive coaches learn how to help athletes make the physical transition back to practice. That is, they learn how to slowly progress their conditioning.
- Coaches who are supportive are consistently supportive of their athletes. Coaches who are consistent demonstrate the same supportive behaviors in practice and competitions. That is, they do not show support in practice and then yell at athletes during games. Coaches who are consistent show the same supportive behaviors in public as they do in private. For instance, they do not show support in front of parents but then demean their players behind closed doors in the locker room during halftime.

- When an athlete misses the game winning shot in basketball, supportive coaches embrace the athlete and use supportive language and remind the team that the last shot does not win or lose the game but rather the collective team performance needs to be considered. A sample supportive statement is, *"While that last shot did not go in, Ken, I am proud of your effort on the court today and how you stepped up and made several shots today that helped put us in a position to win. You are an impact player and I am glad you are a member of our team! Guys, we were so close today – what a game! I am proud of you. You gave good effort and stayed focused throughout the game. We had few turnovers, we rebounded the ball well, and we shot well from the 3 point line. While it is disappointing to lose the game, remember this does not come down to one shot. It is a team game and I think we can all look at our play today and see an area where we can improve. This goes for me, too. When we come back to practice next week, we will continue to work on these areas. Right now, let's huddle up. Everyone on this team is important to our success. Remember, we move forward and upward."*

CLIMATE IN ACTION 3.4

During my time as a collegiate soccer player my coach not only helped me become the best soccer player I could be, he went above and beyond to help everyone on the team develop into the best people we could be. One moment that has always stuck with me was during preseason my sophomore year. Coach asked us to write down one person who we would want to come watch us play, someone who was important to us. During the season before one of our home games, he told us in the locker room that we needed to look into the stands as we warmed up, that there may be some special people here to see us. When we went out to the field I looked and my track coach from high school who had a great influence on me as a runner and athlete was in the stands. It meant so much to me and I was so grateful that Coach took the time to do this for us. It is something I will never forget, and really exemplified how much he cared about his players and the program.

Shared by Morgan Keplinger

Hopefully, what is clear is that support is a tangible action taken by coaches to show they are working on behalf of the athlete. While one athlete might feel supported by recognizing that a coach puts a lot of time and energy into practice, another athlete may feel supported when a coach asks how a doctor's appointment went. The point is that being supportive can take many forms depending on the athlete. Therefore, getting to know the athletes is extremely important to know how best to be supportive. Further, it is important to recognize that supportive actions need to be coupled with good communication so that athletes understand the rationale behind what is happening in practice and how it connects to their respect for them as athletes and wanting to help them get better. We also hope that it is clear that incorporating challenge and intensity in practice is not antithetical to developing a caring environment.

Discipline with Care

Disciplining players is another opportunity for coaches to act with care. We suggest using developmental discipline which is an approach that focuses on nurturing and inviting individuals to develop their own self-control and personal moral standards that help them function as civil and socially responsible individuals within society.[9] The developmental nature of this disciplinary approach calls for a move from power assertions such as strict enforcement of clearly stated rules to open conversations in which individuals learn self-control and social skills and coaches problem-solve with the athlete when poor behavior arises. For example, if an athlete bullies another person on the team, coaches may respond by saying, "*Alana, if this happens again, you're off this team. Do you understand? Do I make myself clear? We don't tolerate behavior like this on our team.*" However, a coach who uses developmental discipline may respond by saying, "*Alana, this is really inappropriate behavior and against our team values. Can you tell me why?* (athlete responds) *Yes, that is right. How would you feel if someone did this to you?* (athlete responds) *I agree, I would feel sad and hurt. Why would you engage in such behavior that makes someone feel hurt and would make them feel sad?*" (athlete responds). How the athlete responds will determine the next course of action. Regardless, the coach tries to act with empathy while still maintaining the consequences for engaging in bullying behavior toward a player (these consequences should be clear to all players at the beginning of the season). However, it is important to help the athlete begin to act differently and to help her see that the coach believes in her ability to act with kindness and respect toward her teammates. Finally, when poor behavior occurs, the best strategy may be to reflect on why the action may have happened and how coaches can alter the environment or circumstances so the behavior will be less likely to occur again in the future. Therefore, the coach may need to understand Alana's life circumstances to know why the bullying happened. However, coaches may also need to consider if they unknowingly condoned bullying behavior.[10]

*****

Developing mutual respect and kindness requires coaches to be intentional in making connections, communicating care, and acting with care. Throughout this chapter, the aim has been to provide a variety of practical suggestions to consider implementing in practice. It is important, however, that coaches reflect on their own personality and coaching style to determine which strategies will work best and how they can be integrated genuinely into their coaching practice. Further, it is important to recognize that while coaches will try to be supportive and care, they will sometimes fall short of this goal. If this happens it is important for coaches to acknowledge their error to the team, learn from the mistake, and seek to act differently in the future. The benefit of a caring and task-involving climate is that when these mistakes happen and coaches own them, the team will act with kindness, respect, and acceptance.

Reflecting on Practice

Part of excellent coaching is reflecting on coaching practice and how it might be improved. Consider the ideas presented in this chapter and reflect upon how you might incorporate them into your own coaching practice. Here are a few prompts to get you started:

- How will I welcome athletes?
- When before, during, or after practice can I set aside time for "getting to know you" conversations?
- What community building activities can I incorporate into the season?
- What activity can I do to let my players know I value their involvement on the team?
- When I think about my team, how do they show care for one another? If I think about each athlete on the team, do they each show care to their teammates? Do they each receive care from their teammates?
- How will I give feedback to the athletes?
- What are the team values for our program?
- What stories can I use throughout the season to reinforce the team values?
- How can I support and care for my athletes? If I went down the roster and thought about each athlete on my team, what would each perceive as caring and supportive behaviors that I can do?

Communities of Practice

Communities of practice occur when a group of people come together with the goal of learning from one another. Within coaching, this entails finding trusted peers to share knowledge and experiences in order to improve your coaching practice. Coaches may have multiple communities of practice that focus on varying aspects of coaching practice (e.g., coaches within sport vs. coaches involved in other sports). We would encourage you to consider finding trusted peers to improve your coaching climate. Here are some ways that community of practice members can be helpful related to this chapter:

- Invite a trusted colleague to your practice to observe your interactions with players and provide thoughts on creating mutual kindness and respect (observations can entail welcoming of players, types of feedback provided, points of listening, missed opportunities to care, etc.). Be sure to return the favor. If it is not possible to have a coach visit your practice, consider video-taping yourself.
- Share with another coach how you disciplined an athlete. Discuss ways in which you did and did not act with care.
- Share with other coaches current events that could provide great teachable moments about mutual kindness and respect.

Sources

1 Hellison, D. (2011). *Teaching personal and social responsibility through physical activity* (3rd ed.). Champaign, IL: Human Kinetics.

2 Carmichael, S. G. (February, 2015). *How to coach, according to 5 great sports coaches*. Harvard Business Review, February, 25, 2015. Retrieved June 5, 2018 from https://hbr.org/2015/02/how-to-coach-according-to-5-great-sports-coaches?referral=03758&cm_vc=rr_item_page.top_right

3 Landtroop, L. (2012). Positive communication, positive results. In D. Hannula & N. Thornton (Eds.), *The swim coaching bible, vol. II* (pp. 320–332). Champaign, IL: Human Kinetics.

4 Reuters (2018, October 9). Roger Federer calls on tennis players to respect ballboys and ballgirls. *The Guardian*. Retrieved from www.theguardian.com/sport/2018/oct/09/roger-federer-calls-on-tennis-players-to-respect-ballboys-and-ballgirls

5 Hoffman, M. & Hoffman, C. (2010, Winter). Hauppauge Middle School and William T. Rogers Middle School: Soccer teams and coaches. *The Bridge*. Retrieved from http://dsafonline.org/wp-content/uploads/2013/09/The-Bridge-december_2010-8.pdf

6 Rapaport, R. (January–February, 1993). *To build a winning team: An interview with head coach Bill Walsh*. Harvard Business Weekly, Retrieved June 5, 2018 from https://hbr.org/1993/01/to-build-a-winning-team-an-interview-with-head-coach-bill-walsh

7 Landtroop, L. (2012). Positive communication, positive results. In D. Hannula & N. Thornton (Eds.), *The swim coaching bible, vol. II* (pp. 320–332). Champaign, IL: Human Kinetics, p. 328.

8 C. G. Jung Quotes. (n.d.) Retrieved from www.goodreads.com/author/quotes/38285.C_G_Jung

9 Watson, M. (2008). Developmental discipline and moral education. In L. Nucci & D. Narvaez *Handbook of moral and character education* (pp. 175–203). New York: Routledge.

10 Baltzell, A. L. & Holt, M. (n.d.). *9 ways coaches can prevent bullying*. Retrieved on June 11, 2018 from https://learn.truesport.org/9-ways-coaches-can-prevent-bullying/.

4

FEATURES OF A CARING AND TASK-INVOLVING CLIMATE IN SPORT

Effort and Improvement are Valued and Recognized

Highlights

- There are many ways for coaches to be creative in highlighting the value of effort and improvement in every aspect of the team.
- Effort and improvement can be emphasized early, throughout, and at the end of the season in both practices and competitions.

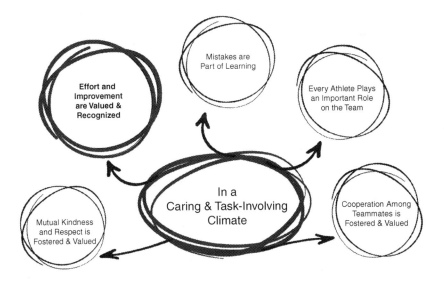

Joe Ehrmann, former college and NFL athlete, and author of *Inside Out Coaching* said, "Youth sport coaches may be the most powerful group of people in the world."[1] This is due, in part, to the potential coaches have to encourage kids to value giving high effort at something in their lives. In fact, one of the most important features of a caring and task-involving climate in youth sport may be coaches' praise and recognition of young athletes' effort and improvement. There is a joy that comes to athletes when they make the decision and follow through on giving their best effort to their pursuits. When young people have nothing that they feel is worth giving their best effort to, it sets them up for an unfulfilling life. If at the end of a sport season, coaches have taught their athletes to value giving consistently high effort, the impact is significant on its own.

In an ego-involving climate, this feature is put on the backseat and replaced with a strong focus on winning and performance outcomes. Coaches who create an ego-involving climate spend most of their words and energy talking to athletes about end results, but research has outlined that the more valuable approach is to aim the bullseye on those factors athletes have control over including effort and improvement across the season.

Helping athletes stay zoned in on giving high effort and monitoring their improvement over time, is key to fostering motivation and helping athletes sustain it over time. So, how can coaches do this? What does this look like in terms of coaches' tactics for effective coaching? The following are strategies that coaches can use to help bolster the message that effort and improvement are at the heart of the team's mission.

It should be noted that what we mean by "high effort" throughout this chapter is probably understood by coaches and athletes. Human beings, in general, seem to have a good sense of the effort they give each day. When coaches and athletes are giving high effort, they are engaged, focused, positive, and determined. It is understood that high effort does not mean athletes are maxing out on their heart rate every second they are in the sport, constantly sprinting in every drill, etc. We are referring to high effort here in terms of both the mental and physical focus.

Strategies to Augment Effort and Personal Improvement with Athletes

- **Start talking about effort and improvement from the first team meeting with the athletes**. Coaches should explain to athletes that success for their team will be centered around hard work and improvement: "*At the end of this season, we are going to look back and measure our success by how hard we worked and how much we improved. Isn't it going to be fun to see where we end up?*" Indeed, effort and improvement are the meters that all coaches should use to gauge the team's success. If the team gives their best effort, regardless of the outcome, athletes are winners. But the words have to be backed up with actions or athletes will quickly realize the inconsistency, and understand that what really matters to coaches is winning and outcomes. We have not come across coaches that do not value high effort (or dismiss its importance), but we have observed many coaches who forget to emphasize it with their athletes. In a task-involving climate, coaches keep effort at the center of their radar screens.

In the Climate in Action 4.1, Hannah Driscoll, a collegiate swimmer, describes how her strength and conditioning coach, Ali Kershner, had a strong focus on personal effort and improvement in the weight room. This focus helped bring out the best of Hannah every session, when she was rested and eager for sessions, as well as when she was fatigued and not at her best.

CLIMATE IN ACTION 4.1

As part of collegiate swimming, our team had weight training three times per week. There were athletes with years of experience in the weight room and others who had never lifted before entering college. Our lifting coach took this into consideration and praised each athlete according to her effort, not by how much she could lift. This was helpful in minimizing the inevitable disappointment and frustration that surfaces when athletes with differing skills and abilities compare themselves to each other. Coach Kershner provided athlete-specific support and stressed the importance of "putting forth YOUR best effort." I recall her walking around the weight room offering encouraging effort- and improvement-based feedback for each individual on the team. As a result of Coach Kershner's focus on effort and improvement, rather than performance and outcome, my desire and drive to reach my potential intensified. Her emphasis on "doing your best" gave me permission to feel good about those sessions where I gave it my all, but did not reach my best performance. Weight training was significantly more enjoyable when I was not worried about lifting more weight irrespective of whether I was sick, stressed or fatigued. In fact, because the emphasis was on showing up, staying focused, and working hard, some of the sessions I went into feeling unmotivated ended up surpassing my expectations. There was a great sense of accomplishment walking out of the weight room knowing I did my best and having my effort recognized by the coach. This gratification inspired me to be fully engaged in every workout. As illustrated by Coach Ali Kershner's actions, a coach who values and recognizes effort and improvement fosters an environment where athletes feel cared for and strive to be the best that they can be.

Shared by Hannah Driscoll

Note: Coach Ali Kershner is an Associate Olympic Sports Performance Coach at Stanford University.

- **Have a team discussion of what effort looks like, both on and off court, and why it is important.** Coaches can bring a chalk/white board or big poster to jot notes of what the athletes say, and ask them questions like this one, "*When is it easy to try hard?*" Coaches will likely get answers from athletes that indicate it is easy to try hard when they are highly skilled/one of the best at the activity, when they are fully rested, or when things are going their way. Coaches should also ask, "*When is it difficult to try hard?*" Athletes will likely share that it is difficult to give full effort when they are losing badly, when they are not as skilled, when they are tired, and/or when they would rather be doing other things. Coaches can write these comments on the white board and lead discussion with the athletes. Everyone understands that it is hard to give best effort all the time, and especially in some of the circumstances mentioned. In fact, not many teams have a full roster of athletes and coaches where every single individual on the team gives consistently high effort.

  Coaches can continue the discussion by asking athletes if they have ever been part of a group or team where everyone is committed to giving their best effort. Coaches can have athletes discuss how special it would be to play on a team where everyone gives maximum effort, and they can explore further what it would look like to be such a team. It is interesting to see what athletes come up with. For example, some athletes may note that a team that gives high effort may never give up when they are down in the game, when they receive bad calls from the officials, when their opponents get lucky on a couple of plays, when the weather is not ideal (really hot or cold), when one of their best players can't play in the competition, etc. If teams have these discussions early in the season and athletes buy into the concept of being a team that gives high effort each day, the coach has much to talk about, reinforce, and celebrate each day thereafter.

  This discussion also gives food for thought to coaches, who can also fall prey to becoming unengaged, giving up, withdrawing effort, going negative, etc. when the team is struggling. If coaches want high effort from athletes, they have to be doing frequent self-checks to be sure they are setting the example for their teams.

  With this discussion, coaches can have athletes think about why they would want effort to be a core value for themselves and their teams. In other words, what are the benefits of giving high effort? Coaches might be surprised to hear athletes talk about how good it feels to know they gave their best effort, to have no regrets, and/or to feel they are people of high integrity.

- **Schedule individual meetings with athletes to discuss their overall development as athletes and teammates**. These meetings would give coaches an opportunity to highlight how the athletes are contributing to the team (e.g., "*Ryan, I love the way you bring energy to practice*"; "*June, your breathing pattern on the flip turn has taken you to a new level*"; "*Mike, it is huge how you are* *focused on supporting your teammates no matter the situation"*; *"Ailis, you are keeping the bat in the zone longer and what a difference that is making"*). Coaches could also emphasize areas that athletes would benefit most from improvement (for example, identifying the open teammate earlier; adding power to the kick; gaining more consistent technique on the jump shot), and help athletes identify drills and activities to work on these aspects of their game. The length and frequency of meetings may depend on the age of the athletes and the level of the sport, but even brief 5-minute meetings could be advantageous. Coaches may have time for these connections with athletes before or after games/practices, or in-between tournament games.

Coaches might have to be creative in thinking about how they can interact with athletes. Maybe they send brief notes, when appropriate, to praise athletes for their effort, note their improvement, encourage them to keep working on a skill, or provide an idea for an activity/drill they could do to work on an aspect of their sport. Perhaps coaches can participate in warmups or cool downs with the team, and this might provide opportunities for brief exchanges with athletes. At early youth sport levels, it may be difficult to squeeze in individual meetings due to limited time for practice and competition, and it may be easier as athletes advance in age and sport level, but at any time, coaches can be mindful of making individual connections with athletes to emphasize strategies for improvement. Coaches should also be aware that they are making sure that every athlete is feeling that coaches are excited and confident in their potential. It is a downer when athletes feel that their coaches are more excited about some athletes compared to others.

- **Be more intentional about structuring every practice around accentuating effort and improvement.** This can be done in many ways, but here are a few examples of how a coach could think about structuring drills that reinforce high effort and improvement.
  - o **Introduction of Drill (Example 1).** Coaches might set up a drill and introduce it with the following words: *"Okay, team, with this next drill we will be working on making crisp passes, moving the ball around the court quickly, and finding the open teammate. We're going to do this drill for 6 minutes and at the end of it I want us to talk about our effort and focus. Our goal is to crank it up a notch and display high effort, just like it was the last 6 minutes of the game. Sound good?"*
  - o **Introduction of drill (Example 2).** *"Okay ladies, in our next drill we are working on back-ups. We need everyone really focused on every situation where they can and need to be backing up a teammate. Let's commit to giving max effort on this; who is with me?"*
  - o **Drill Wrap-Up (Example 1).** At the end of the drill, it is equally important for the coach to come back and discuss the team's effort. Responses could include something like this: *"Guys, what did you think? How focused were we? How was our effort on that drill? How will that kind of*

focus help us on the court in our game this week? I love seeing our improvement in our ability to make those sharp passes and move the ball quickly. We will definitely make mistakes this season, but with this kind of effort there will be fewer mistakes. Great job. Okay, next let's …"

o **Drill Wrap-up (Example 2).** What if a coach shared these words with the team after the drill?: *"It's easy for teams to fall short of providing optimal back-up 100% of the time. If athletes lose focus for a moment or fall into lazy mode, they can fail to provide backup or come in too late. We are a team where that doesn't happen, I think mainly because we have this kind of focus at practice. We are establishing a habit in our brains, like an automatic response. We looked good just now; I love our effort, and our ability to back each other up is going to help us every day of the season. Let's pass some fist bumps around. Okay, next let's …"*

This strategy of setting up a drill to keep the focus on effort brings energy to the group and helps direct athletes' attention. When coaches do not do this and just quickly proceed from one drill to the next, it is easy for athletes' attention to fluctuate, and the overall quality of practice to be diminished.

- **Help athletes create a strong focus on effort at the start of practice.** Young athletes have very busy schedules these days and are involved in many activities. Further, with every athlete, there may be many things going on behind the scenes. Athletes may have considerable homework, and issues at home related to health, finances, and relationships between family members. In addition, they may be working outside jobs or playing multiple sports, or engaged in additional school activities (choir, 4H, debate). A great strategy to help athletes leave the busyness of the day behind them and be able to focus and give high effort at practice is to start each practice with a brief imagery exercise. Coaches might have all the athletes sit on the court/ field, close their eyes, take a couple of deep/full breathes, and speak words such as these …

> The day has probably been busy for each one of us. Since early this morning, our brains have been in high gear. Much of the day we have been at school or work, doing many things, talking to many people, and working on things that will likely continue tonight and into tomorrow. It's easy to let thoughts of these fill our mind during our practice session, but let's see ourselves taking a mental break from all of that. Let's set those things aside for the next 90 minutes and not use energy on them. Instead, let's see ourselves focused on our team. Let's see ourselves giving high effort during this practice … being highly focused … supporting our teammates … let's see ourselves having a great practice that is very productive and that gives us a mental break … a time to do something we really enjoy and be with people who are fun and who make us better. I'm happy to see all of you today. This is one of my favorite parts of the day because I get to spend time with each of you.

Alright, take another two deep breaths and let's start our warmup. [add pause between the sentences to give athletes adequate time to form their images]

Coaches can write their own script and bring in aspects that are specific to their teams. The imagery activity could be shorter or longer depending on the age and needs of the team. The point is that including a short start to practice like this, can help to make athletes more engaged and focused on getting the most out of their time with the team. It would be great if coaches allowed athletes to lead the imagery activity. Athletes could write their own script and it would be motivating to be led by not only coaches but also teammates as the group prepares for practice and/or competitions.

- **Encourage athletes to work hard outside of practice**. One strategy that is underused by coaches is to encourage athletes to work hard outside of practice. Coaches would do well to provide athletes with suggested drills/workouts/activities for practicing their skills outside of their team practice and competitions. It would be helpful if coaches said at the end of practice, "*Hey guys, I think if all of you can commit to play catch with a friend or parent 10 minutes each day this weekend, that will be big for the team. It helps you work on getting your arms in baseball/softball shape so they won't be sore.*"

  One of the roles youth sport can play in society that is badly needed is helping young people be more physically active. Some sports include more physical activity (e.g., soccer, swimming) than others (e.g., baseball/softball). How cool would it be if coaches put little workouts together that young athletes could use to direct their physical activity on off days. It could be a fun way to help youngsters develop their athletic skills, and reap the benefits of adopting a more physically active lifestyle. If coaches encouraged children to be mindful about being physically active 60 minutes a day it could have a huge impact.[2] Coaches could remind kids to get outside, ride their bikes, play with friends, create dance moves, develop new games, make an obstacle course, etc. Coaches could also encourage athletes to practice swinging their racquet (forehand and backhand) or bat using their best technique in their basement/garage/etc. (in front of a mirror). Athletes can leave the cover on their racquet or put a donut on their baseball bat to create greater weight and resistance. An implement feels much lighter after taking off the additional weight.

- **Check-in with the team about everyone's effort after practices and games**. When coaches take time to discuss the level of effort that was displayed at practices and games, it reminds athletes that the importance of effort is huge for the team. Effort is tied to mental skills, being able to sustain focus over time and athletes get better at it with time. A coach can ask the team how they would rate themselves (or the overall team) on their effort in practice or in game. A coach could say, "*Ladies, on a scale of 1–100, how would you rate our team's effort today in the game? How did you arrive at that number?*

What kinds of things did you see us do that reflected high effort? What are areas where you or we (as a team) need to keep working on our effort?"

- **Address unmotivating talk**. One last off the field behavior that is important for coaches to talk about with athletes relates to unmotivating talk. Athletes share with us frequently their frustration in having teammates say things like, *"Uhhhhhg, I wish we didn't have practice today," "I don't feel like playing in a tournament this weekend," "I can't believe we have to play a double-header today"* or *"I wish the season was over."* It is likely that many athletes are not consciously thinking of the impact those negative statements can have for the team, but the fact is that those words show a lack of respect and a disregard for one's coaches and teammates. Further, it creates a mindset that undermines effort. If athletes are wishing they did not have practice today it will be hard to muster effort during practice and may negatively impact their teammates' behavior. Perhaps if coaches led discussions early in the season to help heighten athletes' awareness of their words and the impact they have on them personally and the team, it could help them develop greater maturity and emotional regulation, and understand that giving high effort includes being sensitive to the words they share aloud with their teammates and coaches.

- **Keep the focus on effort and improvement at the end of the season event/wrap-up**. At the end of the season, it is nice to have a ceremony to celebrate everyone's effort and improvement. At ceremonies like this, it is frequently the case that awards are given to athletes who had the best performance statistics. Coaches should give consideration to creating a season-end event that highlights the team's focus on effort and improvement. Perhaps coaches could share a favorite memory of each athlete on the team, one that recognizes these attributes (e.g., *"I'll never forget Jared's hustle from home plate to 1st base, the way he retrieved that ball and how it lead to a double play at that key point in the game. We watched a lot of catchers this season who didn't backup first base, and I appreciate how Jared does it every time."*). Coaches also might print a picture of the team and write a note on the back sharing how much they enjoyed working with each athlete. Together the coaches could identify fun and memorable ways to wrap up the season. Maybe athletes would have great ideas of how to do this as well. The cool thing about this approach is that it is so much better than applauding the few star athletes and the one identified hard-worker.

- **Point out when opponents show these attributes of hard work and note their improvement**. It helps athletes develop respect for their opponents when they realize how fun it is to have opponents (both individually and as teams) who are committed to being the best they can be. Coaches can role model great behavior for their athletes when they build relationships with other coaches, and point out to their own team how opposing coaches and athletes are skilled, work hard, and display class act behaviors. It is fun to coach and compete against others who are held in high regard, and too often in sport opponents are painted as enemies as if all are at war. We are suggesting it is a missed opportunity when coaches are not helping athletes develop a genuine appreciation for their opponents. After all, where would sport be without great opponents (UConn Women's Basketball vs. Notre Dame; Yankees vs. Red Sox; Cowboys vs. Redskins; University of Kansas vs. Missouri; Manchester United vs. Liverpool).

- **Point out the effort that others put in who serve the team in some way.** It is easy for athletes to not be aware of the important role played by the bus driver (or their parents) in transporting them to and from the game; the helpers who lined the fields/prepped the gym; the fans who took time to come and provide their support; the officials who went through extensive training to participate; the league director who put in many hours creating teams and schedules and figuring out numerous organizational details; team parents who put in hours assisting with the needs of the team, etc. The list is long and the efforts of all others should be recognized and appreciated by athletes.

- **Have a mantra reflecting the team's high value of effort.** Some teams might benefit from having a mantra that reinforces their commitment to giving high effort. Athletes can be creative in choosing mantras that have value for them or bring fun to the team. Examples of potential mantras include the following:

  o HEET (i.e., High Effort Everyday, Team). HEET could be a word that athletes and coaches use that is personal for their team, and unknown to others.

  o May the Force be with You (Force = Max effort)

  o No Looking Back (The effort we give today speaks to our mindset)

  o Effort is our Legacy

  o FUNne: FUN w/ Noble Effort

  o LG (Love of the Game)

  Athletes are often more creative than coaches and come up with fun and motivating ideas. It would be beneficial for athletes to have the responsibility to develop core philosophical reminders for a team of the key attributes they want to display daily.

- **Superhero osmosis.** Athletes can display the mannerisms and attributes of Superheroes. A fun strategy to use before or after a practice or game, might be to have the team take the stance of their favorite Superhero and hold that position for 1–2 minutes. For example, Wonder Woman can often be seen with her hands in fists placed on her hips with an upright stance with solid footing. Actually taking the stance and/or imagining taking the stance might serve to help athletes be reminded of how strong and resilient they are. Like Wonder Woman, and all her colleagues (Batman, Flash, etc.), she brings a determination to work hard, and makes the best of every situation she faces.

- **Watch a movie together that highlights high effort.** Coaches can plan for their team to watch a movie together that highlights a person/group who overcome challenges, who give full effort, who show tremendous determination, who are relentless in their work ethic, and whose effort leads to improvement and positive outcomes over time. These movies can be fictional, based on true stories, documentaries, new or older films, etc. Examples to consider might be *A League of Their Own*, *Invictus*, *The Perfect Season*, *Norma Rae*, and *RBG*. Coaches can schedule a gathering with the team to either go to a movie or watch it at someone's house. When watching in a home, it allows the coach to stop the movie every 20-ish minutes to discuss what is happening, what decisions the characters are making, what the athletes would have done if they had been in those situations, and what can be learned and applied to their lives. It is incredibly fun to watch movies with athletes and have a chance to discuss them along the way.

  Coaches might also even consider telling their athletes when they plan to see a movie, and inviting anyone who might be available to join them at the theatre. This would allow for a smaller group to interact and discuss the movie. Maybe the group could meet for smoothies after the movie to discuss it. We recently saw *Won't you be my neighbor?*, a documentary about Fred Rogers, the well-known creator and host of the children's show, Mr. Roger's Neighborhood.[3] Rogers was revolutionary for his approach to interacting with children in a mature, caring style and directly addressing controversial issues of the day. In one episode he invited the local police officer to stop and soak his feet in a shared water bath, at a time when whites were fighting the integration of public swimming pools. This is one example of a film where there is much to talk about the way that athletes (and all individuals) can use their effort to send positive messages and make their team better (and the world a better place).

- **Take athletes on outings that highlight the effort and strength of other individuals/groups**. Coaches could think about taking their athletes on other outings that involve visiting a museum or site (cemetery where famous person is buried; statue of famous event/person/group). Even rural towns often have small museums that may honor and recognize individuals (e.g., fire fighters, farmers, presidents) who have maximized their talents and/ or shared generously with others. In the town of Lawrence, KS there is the Haskell Cultural Center and Museum that highlights the poor treatment of American Indians and their resiliency in overcoming adversity. Lawrence is also home to the Spencer Museum of Art, a small museum on the University of Kansas campus where staff gladly put together sessions for groups (e.g., a team of young athletes) that center around topics of interest (passion for activities [sport]; focus; resiliency). Many young athletes do not have the opportunity to experience rich cultural activities such as these and could benefit on many levels, but a primary one being their exposure to thought provoking concepts about the role that effort and commitment play in sport and life.

- **Read a book or article together.** What a great experience for coaches to read books with athletes and discuss them. This could be done as a team activity. For example, coaches might have their team read, *Elevating Your Game: Becoming a Triple-Impact Competitor* by Jim Thompson, Founder of the Positive Coaching Alliance.[4] The focus of the book is how athletes can make themselves, their teammates, and the sport better. Coaches could pick a book or an article written by or about a coach, athlete, or team where the focus is on those qualities reflected in high effort and commitment. What a great opportunity for athletes to read and discuss such information. Coaches might do this with their entire team, individual athletes, or even small groups of athletes within the team. Other books that might be fun to read as a team include, *Bring Your A-Game* by Jennifer Etnier,[5] *Worldchanging 101* by David LaMotte,[6] *Being Peace* by Thich Nhat Hanh,[7] and *The Book of Joy* by Dalai Lama and Desmund Tutu.[8] Even reading a chapter or two of these books might be perfect for athletes depending on their age and maturity levels.

- **Introduce quotes that reinforce effort.** Coaches can help reinforce athletes' attention to the importance of effort by bringing out quotes on a regular basis, or repeating those quotes over time. David Ralph Abernathy, Martin Luther King, Jr's best friend and cohort in the Civil Rights Movement, said he hoped that at the end of his life he would be worthy of having two words engraved on his tombstone, "I tried."[9] Patricia Russell, a civil rights attorney, said, "You only go around one time, and this ain't no practice run."[10] Quotes such as these give coaches fuel to discuss and encourage athletes to value those who have the same appetite for giving their best efforts in whatever they do. Coaches could even make a poster or banner with words/quotes that reinforce these positive messages for the team. They could make small versions of these banners that athletes post in their lockers, carry in their sport bags, or put in their wallets. These ideas serve to remind athletes of the power of effort in their lives and their capacity to make this world better.

A Focus on Athletes' Health

One area that some coaches might feel is beyond the scope of their attention is athletes' behaviors outside the sport. That is, coaches could feel that their athletes' behaviors that are not directly part of their sport activities fall into the realm of parents, teachers, school administrators, etc. to address. However, coaches have unique relationships with athletes. Many athletes spend more time with their coaches than they do with their families and teachers. Because we recognize what a huge role many coaches play in athletes' lives, we would like to see more coaches encourage athletes to take good care of their physical and mental health. This information could apply to a number of chapters in this book but we have included it here, because when athletes engage in unhealthy behaviors, it can prevent them from giving their best effort to their sport experience, it can preclude their optimal improvement over time, and it can hinder their overall investment and commitment to the sport. We definitely are not suggesting that coaches should take over the parenting role, but we do believe that there is good to be done when coaches are proactive in encouraging athletes to engage in healthy behaviors. As many parents attest, they can use all the help they can get to encourage positive health behaviors with their children.

- **Talk to athletes about sleep and nutrition**. Coaches are in a great position to talk with young athletes about behaviors that might take place off the court but affect the team's performance such as sleep and good nutrition. Athletes who have high commitment to their sport take sleep and nutrition seriously. Coaches can share examples of athletes who eat healthy and make their rest and recovery a priority. Helping athletes develop skills to prepare for games is akin to helping them develop life skills. In a discussion with baseball players about how their first tournament of the season went, they shared that they lost the first game 10–2 but it was really all about the first inning, when the other team scored 8 runs. In discussing their preparation, athletes shared that they had stayed up late playing video games, had not gathered their uniform, etc. the night before, woke up late, and did not have time for breakfast. Athletes also shared their mentality that they all perceived the game was already a loss after the first inning, so they were focused on looking ahead to the next game and trying to refocus. After this discussion, athletes developed a pre-game plan that included the night before. They addressed all the details that they wanted to plan for before their next tournament. They wrote it all down and thought through what time they wanted to go to bed to allow for optimal rest, what time to wake up to allow them to get ready and eat a nutritious breakfast, how to lay out everything they would need so as to reduce the likelihood they would forget something important. They also gave thought to the mental approach they would like to have going into the game. As it was, they perceived that they rolled off the bus, onto the field, and were still half asleep. Teaching athletes to develop intentional habits helps athletes see another side of what is involved in giving one's best effort to a pursuit.
- **Talk with athletes about alcohol and illegal substance use**.[11] Alcohol and substance use are another area of behaviors that coaches might discuss with athletes. One high school coach told us that he no longer has any expectation that his athletes will not drink alcohol and smoke marijuana. These behaviors are so prevalent in the youth culture that he feels his words calling for them to use caution on this front will fall on empty ears. While we would agree that these behaviors are common, we also believe that it is easy for coaches to underestimate the extent to which athletes value their views. Many athletes might not perceive that their drug/alcohol use has anything to

do with their team. They might see these behaviors as ones that occur in their private lives and have nothing to do with their membership on the team. One strategy we wish more coaches used would be to have candid discussions with their athletes about these behaviors. Though athletes might view substance use as harmless and unrelated to their sport performance, they should be made aware of the seriousness of these behaviors. We believe this discussion of substance use is an important one to have with athletes and that it ties in beautifully with thinking about commitment and effort (e.g., that alcohol use can have a negative effect on performance which can demonstrate a lack of commitment to their own success and the team's success). When coaches lead discussion about how athletes would define high or low effort for their team, and athletes are given the opportunity to highlight behaviors that reflect high effort, it is likely that they may mention substance use. If athletes do not mention it, it is still important for coaches to bring it to the discussion. Clearly, a team cannot reach its full potential if athletes are spending their off hours getting high and drunk. At the least, coaches may be helping athletes give greater thought to the impact their off-court behaviors have on their team as well as each individual member.

- **Talk to athletes about healthy relationships.** This is another topic where it is easy for coaches to want to bow out of the discussion and leave it to parents, but we would encourage coaches to look for ways to help athletes learn how to engage in healthy relationships with their peers. Many young athletes are putting the health of themselves and others in jeopardy when they give little thought to the possible outcomes of their behaviors (pregnancy, sexually transmitted infections). In addition, many sport programs are in the spotlight each season because their athletes have been disrespectful towards others. The Harvard men's soccer team, for example, had their season suspended when their tradition of compiling a scouting report describing the sexual attributes of female athletes was made public.[12] As repulsive as this is to consider, there are many ways that young people are learning what it looks like to both show and not show respect for other athletes, coaches, and really all human beings on this planet. Coaches who talk to athletes about these behaviors can provide valuable direction and help athletes learn to respect others as well as avoid the pitfalls of learning lessons the hard way. Clearly, a team cannot be all it can be (be all in with effort) when athletes are not treating everyone with kindness and respect. When coaches lead discussion and emphasize to athletes how much they value this concept of respecting others, it may empower athletes to speak out when they observe teammates being disrespectful of others.

- **Educate and empower athletes to discuss and identify signs of eating disorders and depression/suicide.** Too many young athletes struggle with issues such as depression/suicide and disordered eating behaviors/eating disorders. These are difficult issues that require professional help, but coaches who talk about these issues with their teams may be helping their athletes notice the signs and recognize when they or their teammates may need some help. It's easy for athletes to think they are being good friends when they help teammates hide serious behaviors, but coaches can help athletes see that good friends care deeply about one another and want to do all they can to engage in caring behaviors.

Strategies for Emphasizing Athletes' Improvement

Another major aspect of a caring and task-involving climate that goes along with effort is improvement. Humans, in general, can be hard on themselves and easily focus more on their weaknesses and limitations, than their potential for growth. As a result, helping young athletes recognize both their improvement and their potential for improvement, is one of the most important roles that youth sport coaches play. The following are strategies that coaches could use to help athletes stay cognizant of their constant improvement.

- **Create drills that highlight improvement over time.** Coaches can be mindful of incorporating drills that will help athletes see their own and their teammates' improvement over time. Here are a couple of examples of volleyball drills:
  o **Drill 1**: See how many seconds/minutes it takes the team to hit 25 serves in the court (or 10 or 50 or whatever number may be appropriate for the skill level of the team). Line up half the team on the baseline and let the other half of the team shag (or let the parents or coaches shag balls) and see how quickly the team can get a total of 25 serves in the court (athletes are serving at the same time). If coaches log their improvement over practices, it would be fun to see the time needed to hit 25 serves in the court decrease as the team improves, and the delight in the team as they work together on this task.
  o **Drill 2**: Again, athletes are lined up on the baseline, and every athlete serves 15 balls, and keeps track of the number of consecutive serves she can get in. If, for example, an athlete gets 4 serves in a row in the court, and misses one, she starts over until she misses again or has served a total of 15. Athletes report the highest number of consecutive hits they had (during their string of 15 serves) and the totals for the entire team are added up to get a team total. Maybe Candace had seven, Whitney had three and Theresa had five; these add up to 15 (all the athletes' totals would be included). This number will rise as the team improves, and it's a fun way to add focus to a drill and keep the emphasis on the team effort. Those athletes who are the most talented in serving may be able to provide tips and support for others. If Candace is hyped for being

the best, the benefit of the drill has not been achieved, as the purpose is to show the team how everyone's improvement contributes to the overall success of the team. Further, the goal is that athletes are becoming more consistent and confident in their personal ability to nail serves. These kinds of drills provide coaches many opportunities to highlight for the team how small improvements by individual athletes add up to big improvements when considering the team.

o   **Drill 3**: Set up a drill where athletes get points for hitting into different sections on the court. They hit five serves and total their score. This court could be set up before and after practice where athletes can get additional practice. Athletes are encouraged to keep the focus on their own effort and improvement, and it is unimportant which athlete achieves the highest score. The team will benefit as each athlete comes closer to reaching his/her own potential. These drills can easily be adapted to fit the sport, skill level, and needs of coaches and athletes.

These examples of drills focus on improvement with regard to outcome, but coaches can also create drills that focus on technique, such as tracking quality at-bats, better form on strokes (keeping head still or elbow up), and more consistent flip-turns. These kinds of drills would help athletes see how their hard work is resulting in better technique over time.

CLIMATE IN ACTION 4.2

In high school, my freshman year basketball coach [Megan Schnee] had the biggest impact on my sport experience that whole season. She noticed my improvements and highlighted them even when I did not notice the new skills I had gained. She knew that I was not the most comfortable with taking the ball down the court during a game, but she pushed me to so that I would get better. Her confidence in me made me even more confident in myself and my abilities. When I would have a turn over trying to take the ball to the paint or air ball a shot, she would always give me constructive comments and valued my effort in that play. Without her creating an environment where efforts and improvements are valued and recognized, I would not have had the confidence to try new things and attempt new plays.

Shared by Anna Hegarty

•   **Remember to chart progress**. Another strategy that coaches can use to help athletes recognize their improvement is to write things down. One of the reasons that athletes fail to recognize their improvement over time is that it becomes a blur when they do not have tangible evidence. If athletes rely on their memory to note their improvement, there is a good chance they will fail to realize how much ground they cover over time. One of the best ways to keep athletes' improvement in the forefront of their minds is to write things down or find a way to keep a record of their improvement. For example, athletes might track how many kicks they can make at a certain distance and hit the goal, how many crosscourt forehands they can hit consecutively without a miss, how many free throws or left-handed layups they can make in a row? Coaches can encourage athletes to keep track of these things. They might keep a running tally posted in their locker at school or attached to their bathroom mirror or by their bed at home. When athletes are not guided to see their personal improvement, it is easy for them to focus on how they are doing compared to others, and that is not nearly as helpful or motivating as it is to see their personal improvement that has resulted from their high effort. It is especially problematic if athletes are focused on the ways in which other athletes may be better/more advanced (*My friend, Richard, can do 15 pull-ups and I've just worked up to 2*); this can result in frustration and a decline in motivation. Other athletes may have had more resources (e.g., private lessons; better coaching) and longer to reach their current level. However, if all athletes can be directed to focus on their own effort and improvement, the stage is set for them to feel empowered as they monitor their personal improvement.

- **Seek suggestions from athletes**. Another important strategy for coaches who want to help their athletes achieve their potential is to elicit ideas from athletes for drills, how to structure practice, and how to add variety to help the team improve.

  o **Coaches might ask questions for their needs**. "*What do we need to practice more?*" Athletes might give answers like, "*What can we do to keep the ball away from one really talented athlete?*"; "*Can we work on throw downs to 2nd*" (shortstop/2nd base players may not be in position early enough to receive the throw); "*We aren't backing up plays; We are not hitting our cut-off player often enough and it's costing us runs.*" This gives the coach the opportunity to hear directly from athletes, to gain an understanding of their perspective, and send a strong message to athletes that the coach values their input for how to improve the team.

  o **A coach might ask the team for suggestions**. "*How can we use practice time more efficiently? You know, still have fun, but also have intensity and focus?*" Athletes might provide suggestions like the following:

    ■ Edith: "*We can talk about the next drill while we are having a water break*" (instead of losing 5 minutes to athletes just standing around);

    ■ Ches: "*What if we took turns arriving early to practice to get everything set up? That might save us 10 minutes*";

    ■ Queenie: "*What if we turned on great motivating music at the end of practice and timed ourselves to see how quickly we could put all the equipment away. That might save us another 10 minutes of time that could be better spent.*"

■ Walter: "*Why don't we all commit to having better focus when the coach is describing a drill? It seems like it takes a lot longer than it should because some of us zone out and the drill has to be explained several times.*"

All of these are examples of how athletes, even at young ages, can play a key role in helping the coach identify strategies to maximize practice and thus the athletes' sport experience. If ideas come from athletes, they may be more receptive to implementing them and they could result in greater improvement over time.

An interesting example of this at a higher level of sport occurred with the New Zealand All Blacks rugby team. They have been one of the most successful sport teams in the world over the past century. One of the keys to their success is that the coaches allow athletes to be important decision makers for the team. An example of this is when the team captain, Tanna, shared with the head coach that the team felt the coach's pre-match speeches were not helpful and not the best use of the team's time prior to the start of a game. While this was hard for the coach to swallow, upon reflection he realized Tanna was right.

CLIMATE IN ACTION 4.3

[Tanna was] dead right, it was their time. They needed to focus on what they needed to do. They didn't need some other bugger yelling in their ear ... I had been team-talking for 30 years, and I thought it was bloody important, and he thought it was a bloody waste of time ... He was dead right, and thank God he told me. I could still be doing it.

Shared by Graham Henry (New Zealand All Blacks rugby coach)[14]

• **Help parents understand how to help their athletes develop skills.** Coaches might also reflect on how they can assist parents to help their children grow as athletes. Coaches might, for example, create handouts that parents can use to help their child work on skills. Along these lines, they could identify the key cues for a skill, such as learning to throw a ball overhand (position of hand on ball, step with opposite foot than throwing hand). This helps parents see what cues are involved in the skill, and they may be less likely to guide young athletes down the wrong path of skill development. Even better, parents may be able to give their children helpful feedback (e.g., your body went straight up on that jump shot; awesome job!; great footwork as you rounded 2nd base) and provide technical and emotional support that make the athlete better and strengthens the relationship with their parents. This suggestion is not for parents to take over the role as coaches, but that parents can have a better idea of the skills athletes are working on, not do harm to their development by giving the wrong cues, and perhaps help out a little (e.g., by providing another set of eyes, filming the athlete do a skill) by reinforcing improvement. One parent appreciated how her daughter's lacrosse coach provided links to videos that parents could watch to learn more about the sport. When coaches use these strategies, they can help parents help their sons and daughters develop an approach to sport that is focused on learning, improving, and developing as athletes.

- **Sherlock Moments.** Another way to help athletes see their improvement and the improvement of their teammates is to have a "Sherlock Moment" after practice. The name comes from the popular detective, Sherlock Holmes, who picked up on the tiniest details of a case. In fact, nothing got by Sherlock. In a similar vein, coaches want their athletes to be versions of Sherlock when it comes to seeing improvement in themselves, their teammates, and the overall team. During the Sherlock Moment, athletes have a chance to speak about the improvements they are noting in all these cases. It can be an energizing and positive way to end practice. In fact, what could be more valuable than taking a few moments, as a team, to note improvement in self, teammates, and possibly even coaches! Athletes are often slow to recognize their own personal improvement but may take to heart comments from coaches and teammates who are noticing their improvement and verbalizing positive comments for all to hear. Athletes who learn to compliment others are developing an important communication skill that helps in all aspects of life.

Additional Notes about Emphasizing and Valuing Effort and Improvement

- **Praise of one athlete does not need to come at the expense of another athlete.** One thing we notice coaches doing at times is praising some athletes at the expense of others. For example, we have heard coaches in their post-game talks say something like this after a loss, "*I can't tell that anyone on this team cares. I know Simmons cares … I know Ruiz cares … but I can't tell about the rest of you.*"

  The coach then goes on a diatribe with a lot of negative information, stemming from frustration over a loss. There is a high likelihood that the coach does not really believe that no athlete or only two athletes on the team care. Athletes who have given high effort and hear these words from a coach can feel discouraged. It is important for coaches to understand that this approach does not result in positive outcomes; rather, it drains energy from the team and creates a downward vibe. If there were one strategy that would benefit coaches, we feel like this may be it. **If coaches could realize that they never have to praise and recognize effort and improvement in one athlete at the expense of another, sport could look very different.**

In this example, it should be noted that the coach demonstrates a lack of ability to regulate his/her emotions. When frustrated, it can be challenging to rope in emotions, and in this case, the coach would be better off demonstrating an ability to look more objectively at the team's performance and find ways to highlight the good things that happened and inspire the team to be better in the next game. That would reflect effective coaching and show the team how to respond in a more positive way moving forward.

- **Brainstorm how to spread the team philosophy that effort and improvement are the focus.** Coaches could brainstorm how to share their primary focus of effort and improvement on the team with athletes, parents, fans, media, officials, and all who are involved in sport. Coaches can discuss their approach at parent meetings early and throughout the season, provide inserts in the roster sheets/programs provided at competitions, have announcements made over the loudspeaker, etc. The more that all involved parties are exposed to the approach, the better for sport. Aubrey Newland, a sport psychology professional, identified another good idea for how a team's philosophy could be highlighted. She suggests that coaches, athletes, and/or parents could create a short video that describes the team's focus on effort and improvement. What a creative idea for getting those most closely invested in the team to think outside the box, and come up with a fun video.

- **The meaning of competition.** Sometimes people interpret Nicholls' theory as suggesting that competition is bad and should be avoided, or that athletes should not care about winning. This is completely inaccurate, as striving to win is at the core of sport. Athletes cannot measure their improvement without being in challenging situations where they can see their improvement over time. Really, it is impossible to improve as an athlete without competing often against others. The point is that the joy of competition should come from striving to be one's best against the most challenging of competitors, more so than demonstrating that one is better than others.

- **Emphasize effort and improvement early in the season.** Many coaches may assume that athletes are naturally focused on their effort and improvement and may not realize how important it is to generate discussion early in the season to be sure everyone understands the team's philosophy. When coaches do not emphasize these features early in the season, it may cause teams to start out slow, to not work as hard, and to be less concerned with their own and their teammates' improvement. Not talking about effort and improvement can set teams up to have athletes that are more worried about their own performance in comparison to others rather than the team's overall success. Many teams begin to bond as the season progresses and come closer to reaching their potential as time goes by, but they miss out on achieving the team's potential.

- **The role of athletes in a climate focused on effort and improvement.** When the coach makes the goal of every athlete giving maximal effort and striving to reach his/her potential, it changes the role of teammates. They go from being rivals and adversaries who are trying to best one another, to teammates who are trying to push one another to be the best they can be, which all contributes to helping the team be the best it can be. Teammates should be supportive allies, not wary adversaries.

*****

Athletes are fortunate when they have coaches that focus their attention on effort and improvement. This approach helps athletes tune in to the most important aspects of sport that will guide their commitment and sustain their motivation over time. Emphasizing effort and improvement is well supported by theory and research, and it may be the greatest gift coaches can give their athletes.

Reflecting on Practice

Effective coaching involves reflecting on your behaviors and approach to coaching and how they might be improved. Consider the ideas presented in this chapter and reflect on how you currently emphasize effort and improvement in your coaching practice, and how you might incorporate strategies that could further help your athletes.

Effort

- To what extent does my team feel that effort is valued above performance and outcome (winning)? [I could ask athletes about this to gain their feedback.]
- What strategies, behaviors, and/or words are helping reinforce that message?
- What are other ways that I could strengthen athletes' understanding of the importance of effort on our team?
- What strategies could I use to highlight the value we place on effort that are specific to practice, competitions, preseason, and/or postseason activities?
- What strategies and ideas from the chapter am I excited to try out with my athletes that will help emphasize effort?

Improvement

- Currently, to what extent do my athletes perceive that I notice and value their improvement? [I could ask athletes about this to gain their feedback.]
- How do I demonstrate to the team that improvement is important to me and to each athlete?
- What additional strategies, behaviors could I use to highlight their improvement in all aspects of the sport (skills, strategies, teamwork, effort, mental skills, etc.)?
- How do I encourage my athletes to give positive feedback to each other that will make them better?
- What strategies and ideas from the chapter am I excited to try out with my athletes that will showcase their improvement?

Opportunities to Observe, Discuss with, and Learn from Others

- Coaches might ask the league director to include effort/improvement as a topic for discussion at a league coaches' meeting. What strategies do other coaches use to emphasize effort and improvement? What mistakes have they made/lessons have they learned?
- Coaches can pair up with a coach and trade observations of their practices and competitions. High School principal Ron Abel allows teachers to create their own in-service day to go and spend a day at another school observing

another teacher/coach. Teachers share their delight in being able to make a new connection with a colleague or observe a good friend's program. They describe how they come away with new ideas and insights. In a similar manner, collaborating with a coach of another team or league could be stimulating. A coach might attend a practice and/or be in the dugout/on the sideline for a game, and it could be a great learning experience for all.

- Coaches might seek feedback from athletes to see their perceptions of how much athletes think effort and improvement are the most valued qualities of the team, and how those qualities could be better reinforced.

Sources

1   Ehrmann, J. (2011). *Inside-out coaching: How sports can transform lives.* New York, NY: Simon and Schuster.

2   Center for Disease Control. *Youth physical activity guidelines* (Retrieved April 19, 2019): www.cdc.gov/healthyschools/physicalactivity/guidelines.htm

3   Neville, M. (2018). *Mr. Rogers: Won't you be my neighbor?* Documentary by Focus Features: Comcast.

4   Thompson, J. (2011). *Elevating your game: Becoming a triple-impact competitor.* Portola Valley, CA: Balance Sports.

5   Etnier, J. L. (2009). *Bring your 'A' Game: A young athlete's guide to mental toughness.* Chapel Hill, NC: University of North Carolina Press.

6   LaMotte, D. (2014). *Worldchanging 101.* Montreat, NC: Dryad.

7   Hanh, T. N. (2005). *Being peace.* Berkley, CA: Parallax Press.

8   Lama, D. & Tutu, D. (2016). *The book of joy.* New York: Avery.

9   Abernathy, R. D. (Retrieved April 19, 2019): https://quoteshype.com/Authors/Ralph_Abernathy

10 Russell, P. (Personal communication, June 20, 1978).

11 National Strength and Conditioning Association. The effects of alcohol and athletic performance. (Retrieved April 19, 2019): www.nsca.com/education/articles/nsca-coach/the-effects-of-alcohol-on-athletic-performance/

12 The Guardian. *Harvard ends men's soccer team season over lewd rankings of female players.* (Retrieved April 19, 2019). www.theguardian.com/education/2016/nov/04/harvard-men-soccer-team-season-lewd-rankings-female-players

13 Madison, K. (2019, March–April). Matt Bragga: Havin' fun and gettin' it done. *Inside Pitch*, 18–20.

14 Hodge, K., Henry, G., & Smith, W. (2014). A case study of excellence in elite sport: Motivational climate in a world champion team. *The Sport Psychologist*, 28, 60–74.

5

FEATURES OF A CARING AND TASK-INVOLVING CLIMATE IN SPORT

Mistakes are Part of Learning

Highlights

- Coaches can benefit from taking a deep look at how they respond to their athletes' mistakes.
- When coaches respond to athletes' mistakes with punishment, athletes can then respond in a way that actually impairs their performance.
- Understanding why mistakes can occur in sport is key to being an effective coach.
- Teaching athletes to treat mistakes as avenues for learning is a game-changer.

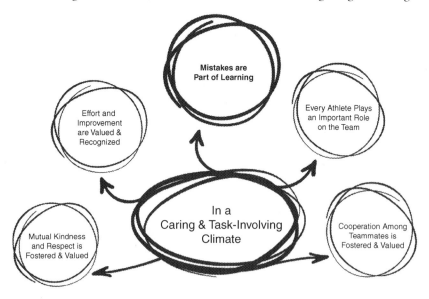

The next feature of a caring and task-involving climate addresses how coaches should respond when athletes make mistakes, and the goal is to treat mistakes as part of the learning process. We live in a sport world where we often see athletes called out for mistakes in a very direct, embarrassing way, and it is easy to think that punishing mistakes is the best way to get athletes' attention and help them stop making mistakes. However, we have considerable research and experience observing this to know that this is not the case. When coaches help athletes frame mistakes as part of their continued growth and development it changes their entire perspective and sets them up to work harder to improve and to push to achieve more challenging tasks.

CLIMATE IN ACTION 5.1

As you begin this chapter, stop for a moment and think about mistakes you've made in the past and how coaches responded to you. What reactions were helpful and which were not helpful? How did you respond when a coach yelled and screamed versus spoke to you in a calm manner and treated you like a human being? What feedback helped you focus on the next play or see your long-term potential? What feedback made you feel that you should give up the sport or spend more time on the bench? Your reflection on your own experiences with making mistakes in sport will be valuable as you consider this chapter.

Why Teach Athletes that Mistakes are Part of Learning?

When we think about it, it makes a lot of sense because when athletes are taught that mistakes are part of learning they …

- Can focus on correcting the mistake without the distraction of incoming punishment (e.g., being yelled at; running laps);
- Are more likely to take risks and try new and creative things, which is basic to learning;
- Are less likely to tense their muscles or worry about the mistake;
- Are less likely to develop a fear of making mistakes that can be paralyzing (i.e., keeps athletes in their bubble, playing it safe);
- Are more likely to focus on the moment (exactly what coaches want them to do, right?) rather than the past (e.g., "*I just messed up*") or the future (e.g., "*I hope I don't mess up again*");
- Feel more free to play assertively and go for plays and do the things that will help their team (i.e., and not play safe to avoid mistakes);

- Are more likely to extend themselves, play creatively, and break through to the next level (do the things athletes have to do to move to the next level);
- Become better teammates because they are focused on helping themselves and others move beyond a mistake;
- Begin to realize that all great athletes are great because they made 100s of mistakes along the way and persisted to keep getting better, so really, if athletes aren't making mistakes, it is likely that they are not pushing themselves hard enough.

Look at the all-time leader board for strikeouts in MLB baseball, missed shots in NBA basketball, most interceptions in the NFL, etc., and you will find that it is filled with some of the best players who ever played the game. It is easy to forget that these great athletes made so many mistakes along the way. It is definitely not what we remember about them.

As described above, while there are great reasons not to adopt the philosophy of punishing mistakes, there are even more and better reasons for teaching athletes that mistakes are part of learning. When athletes can consider mistakes as avenues for growth, the door is opened for them to develop their athletic potential. Helping athletes adopt this view of mistakes as learning opportunities can be challenging from both coaches' and athletes' perspectives. Many coaches have never experienced this approach in either their years as athletes or their tenure as coaches. Dan and Tom, introduced in Climate in Action 5.2, are two examples of coaches who had been involved in sport for years as athletes and coaches before they ever questioned that creating an ego-involving climate was not the best approach when trying to bring out the best in athletes.

CLIMATE IN ACTION 5.2

Dan was part of a collegiate football coaching staff who decided to commit to creating a caring and task-involving climate after years of creating an ego-involving climate.[1] He said,

"You know I played at Haskell my freshman year. The coach was in my tail all the time. We would be watching film and he would be chewing me out. He'd be embarrassing me in front of the entire team and that was his way of motivating me to be better. I had to walk on eggshells. I had to do everything perfect. You know and I was a freshman and it was very hard to do it like that, but I learned quick … A lot of the stuff we are talking about now, about not chewing out a kid, about always using positive reinforcement, that's new for me, that's a totally new technique. That's a totally new area that I have never seen, that I have never practiced, that I have never been exposed to."

CLIMATE IN ACTION 5.2 Continued

After being part of a coaching staff that committed to creating a more caring and task-involving climate for their football team, Dan had this to say:

"*It has made all the difference for me. I have such a better relationship with my players. I feel like they are more bought into the system. I feel like it's easier for me to talk to them on a football level, but also on a personal level about life, about their classes, about, you know, societal things, whatever it might be. Whatever might be bothering them, you know, they are so much more open to me. Whereas years in the past, being more of an old school kind of hard-ass mentality, it tended to push more kids away than anything else.*"

Dan's fellow coach, Tom, added this about their athletes' responses to the coaches' new philosophy and efforts to create a caring and task-involving climate:

"*Early on I think that they appreciated it and maybe it was, it created an environment where a kid could go 100% and not worry about making a mistake. He can play maybe a little more free, his performance could be a little more free, and he wouldn't hold himself down because he was scared to make a mistake, or scared to be pulled out of the game.*"

Even if coaches buy-in to the approach that mistakes should be treated as part of the learning process, they may still get caught up in the moment and sometimes revert back to the mindset that mistakes are bad and must be punished. And even if coaches are totally sold on the approach, they may have athletes who have never been helped to view mistakes in this way. Many athletes are hard on themselves and quick to feel that they need to be punished and/or beat themselves up after every mistake. So, coaches have to be intentional in getting full buy-in from athletes to adopt the approach that mistakes are part of learning, and coaches must realize the huge role they play on this front.

Understanding Why Athletes Make Mistakes

Often coaches get upset in practice because they observe their athletes failing to make crisp passes, back up their teammates, catch passes, get a quick start off the starting line, etc., and responses are often to get upset, rant and rave, throw a mini-tantrum, and punish athletes. However, one of the most effective coaching practices that can occur is for coaches to thoughtfully break down why these mistakes are made and even ask athletes to reflect on why they think they keep making those mistakes. However, regardless of the reasons why mistakes happen, it is important for coaches to adopt an approach to helping athletes overcome mistakes, develop the skills needed to make the mistakes less often in the future, and become more resilient in how they respond to mistakes. In each case, going down a negative road is not likely to help an athlete overcome mistakes as much as going positive. First, it is important to take a look at some of the reasons why athletes make mistakes.

- **Poor technique**. The number one reason athletes make mistakes (i.e., particularly in youth sport) is probably because they have not developed strong technique. That is, they need to keep working on consistently utilizing the cues (bend knees, follow-through, pick up on placement of opponents more quickly, etc.) that will make their performances more consistent over time. As straightforward as this appears to be, it seems that many coaches, instead of chalking up mistakes to poor or less developed technique, point the finger at effort or lack of ability. In this case, coaches would do well to take a deeper look and to help athletes understand that mistakes are part of the process, and they just need to keep working hard to become more consistent in their performance.

  Along these lines, coaches need to recognize that opponents play a key role in athletes' performances as well. As athletes compete against more skilled opponents, it can affect their ability to perform consistently, as the pressure is greater. Take, for example, a young volleyball team that is still working on getting serves in the court consistently, and they play against a team where a number of athletes are doing jump serves. It is sometimes the case that the team may have more errors on serving, suggesting they are feeling the pressure of playing against a more skilled team. Coaches would do well to break down what may be the root cause of the errors, and find a way to provide encouragement to their athletes.

- **Lack of focus**. Athletes sometimes make mistakes because they have not adequately developed the mental skill of being able to sustain their focus over an extended period of time. They may zone out for a moment, forgetting to look for the open receiver, track the baserunner, keep track of the time on the clock, etc. Coaches can often chalk these mental mistakes up to a lack of effort, but it is important to realize that focus is a mental skill that requires practice. Coaches turning negative is not likely to help athletes further develop their focus skills, but providing encouragement, being understanding, and developing ways that they can enhance their focus are key strategies coaches can use to help their athletes treat mistakes as learning opportunities.

- **Lack of confidence/anxiety/fear of making a mistake**. Another cause of mistakes by athletes is their nervousness about making a mistake, letting the team down, and fear of being embarrassed/humiliated in front of others. Mistakes such as these can come from a lack of confidence, anxiety, and/or fear of making mistakes. These thoughts can be extremely distracting for athletes, and easily explain how youngsters can be prone to making mistakes in practice and even more-so in competitions. If coaches respond with negative comments and body language to these kinds of mistakes, the effects on athletes are likely to be debilitating. Instead, if coaches reassure athletes that they believe in them, that the consequences of making a mistake are not dramatic, and reinforce the team's approach to addressing mistakes as avenues for learning, pressure is released for athletes. Athletes would know and feel that they have a foundation of support sitting right on their bench.

Here's an example of a coach that did not handle mistakes well in a match with her youth volleyball team, and suggestions for how her responses may have been more effective.

o **The situation**: Her team is playing in a volleyball tournament where the opposing team is much better than her recreational team athletes. In this match, her team is getting pounded. She calls a time-out and proceeds to shred her athletes, saying …

What is wrong with you (coach has blood vessels popping out of her throat as she is talking and obviously is in a bad mood)? *You look like imbeciles on the court. You're not ready to return serves, your hits are pathetic, and you act like you don't care. This is embarrassing and I've got better things to do than be here on a Saturday morning if you're going to play like this. Get your butts out there* (She didn't even do a hands in the circle breakdown before sending the athletes back on the court).

The coach, as we might imagine, did not help her athletes in this situation. Her athletes looked like deer in headlights. They lacked focus and confidence, and fun was nowhere to be found on their side of the court. So what if the coach had thought more carefully about her words and why her athletes were making mistakes, and what if she had responded in this manner?:

Ladies (coach is smiling and has arms open to welcome athletes to the circle), *whew, we are playing a good team. They have been playing longer than many of you and have had a chance to develop their technique. They serve harder than we do today and it's challenging for us because we usually have more time to react to the serve coming over the net. It seems to me we have a choice to make. We can either say they are too good for us, and we just fold, or we can say, "What a great opportunity for us to be challenged!" Our goal is to get the most out of this match. How do we do that? Let's crank our focus up a little bit, let's get in ready position sooner so that we're ready to pick up on the serve, and let's stay determined every point. Let's support each other like crazy, and let's dismiss mistakes so when a mistake happens let's just get ready for the next point. I think we are better than we know, and I think the other team might think they're a little better than they are, so let's see how close we can hang with them. Let's give this all we have. What do you think? Okay, let's get out there and embrace the challenge* (she does a hands in the circle breakdown before sending them out).

Regardless of whether athletes were making mistakes because their technique was poor, they struggled to focus in the match, or they were experiencing stress about making mistakes, the words of the coach would be more effective in the second response. The coach offered encouragement, technical instruction, and a perspective. Her team was not likely to win this match but they could definitely use it as a learning experience.

- **Self-fulfilling prophecy.** Another angle to consider that connects to athletes making mistakes is linked to the self-fulfilling prophecy. Research has revealed that sometimes coaches can form an impression of an athlete early on that is inaccurate but leads the coach to form an expectation for the athlete.[2] If coaches convey their expectations to athletes, and athletes pick up on the expectations and conform to them, it can, in some cases, lead to athletes failing to reach their potential, particularly if the expectations are for low performance. For example, if a coach has three athletes that play the center position in basketball and judges that the shortest/smallest of the three is likely to be the least skilled, it might lead the coach to act in ways that send messages to all three athletes that there is a hierarchy, and expectations are highest for the bigger/taller of the three athletes. The danger occurs if the smaller/shorter athlete internalizes the expectations of the coach and begins to expect that he/she is less skilled than the other two and will never perform up to their level. In some cases, the smaller/shorter athlete might have a higher skill level, but could start to doubt him/herself due to the coach's low expectations. Another danger of this situation is that the taller/bigger athletes may begin to realize the coach believes they have higher ability, and they might feel they don't need to work as hard because they are already the favored athletes of the coach. Coaches should check the expectations they form for athletes, and always ensure that they are not sending messages to athletes that suggest their lack of confidence in their potential to improve. One athlete told us his coach pulled him from the lineup of a game at the beginning of the season and told him, "*Hey, Mario, I wanted to put Peter in to pinch hit because I thought he could hit a double.*" Peter struck out in three pitches, but the point is that the coach's words undermined confidence of the athlete. If the coach had said, "*Mario, listen, I didn't pull you because I lacked confidence in your ability; I'm just trying to get different guys into the game and Peter hasn't had an opportunity yet. I know how capable you are, Mario,*" it would have conveyed a completely different message to the athlete. Many athletes share with us their experience of coaches saying things that make their confidence take a hit. Often, athletes are speaking about being smaller and facing assumptions from coaches that bigger, taller framed athletes are more experienced and talented.

CLIMATE IN ACTION 5.3

It is important for coaches to think about the effect their responses have on athletes who may be making mistakes for any of the reasons above. For example, take an athlete who is playing shortstop and bobbles an easy grounder that should have been a double-play ball but results in no outs on the play at a key point in the game.

> **Coach**: *You have got to make that play!!* (yelling, kicks over a bucket in the dugout)
>
> OR
>
> **Coach**: *You're okay, Jessica/Jake. Remember to stay down on the ball. You got this. Let's all refocus. One out, let's get the lead runner if possible.*

Making Mistakes Part of Learning

Here are some strategies to consider for how coaches can help their athletes embrace the concept that "mistakes are part of learning" and some examples of coaches' experiences that we can all learn from.

- **Punishment is not the answer.** Regardless of why the athlete made the mistake (e.g., poor technique, lack of focus, anxiety/lack of confidence), a negative response from the coach is not likely to be helpful for the athlete who made the mistake or the rest of the team. The coach's negative response may even help the opposing team as they may think they now have the upper hand and are playing against a divided team. When coaches respond with negative behavior after a mistake it sometimes gives the impression they think athletes made mistakes on purpose because they simply do not care. However, it is not likely that many young athletes think it would be amusing to make a crucial mistake in front of teammates, opponents, and fans. It is hard to imagine that many athletes simply do not care in this situation, and it is much more likely that the vast majority of mistakes are made because athletes need to keep working on their technique, knowledge of the game, and their mental skills. Coaches need to remind themselves that athletes are young, and mistakes are expected.
- **Responding to athletes' mistakes with maturity.** Finally, if coaches believe that athletes are not giving full effort, we maintain that punishment is not the answer, but instead, this situation calls for one-on-one genuine discussion. That is, coaches should speak directly to athletes and share their perceptions. It may appear to the coach that an athlete is not trying hard,

but it is important to delve deeper. Maybe the athlete's grandfather was diagnosed with cancer yesterday, or maybe the athlete is losing interest in the sport, is pulled in many directions, is not getting sleep, is struggling in school, lacks friends, or one of 200 other reasons why athletes may withdraw effort. Coaches should talk to athletes and it is okay to share their own perceptions in a candid way such as this, *"Angie/Kip, I want to talk to you and be honest with you. It looks to me like you are not giving your best effort to the team. At practice, I perceive that you don't try your hardest and I wanted us to have a chance to talk about it. It's really frustrating for me because I see how your lack of effort affects the entire team, and I want to understand what's going on. Am I right, is that accurate, or am I missing something? Do you feel like you are giving your best effort? I really want to understand your views on this."* So often coaches react with punishment in these situations, but how much more logical and powerful for a young athlete to have a coach who will take time to delve deeper into the situation, value obtaining the athletes' view, and display such a caring approach.

CLIMATE IN ACTION 5.4

I've been on teams where you were punished if you made a mistake ... didn't matter if it was a physical or mental mistake. The bottom line was that you were running poles if you messed up. That wasn't the case on this team [high school summer league]. My teammates and I were 17 years old. We were well aware when we did something wrong, but instead of my coach [Scott Jones] yelling at us and punishing us, he turned everything into a learning experience. One time during practice we were working on our situation bunt defense schemes. Our catcher signaled the scheme to the infield and I ended up in the wrong position. After the play was over, my coach asked me what happened. After explaining to him that there was confusion with the signaling, we ended up switching signals for each scheme in order to have more clarity. If this was an ego-involving climate, I would have been punished for making a mistake, but we also probably wouldn't have changed signals. Instead, my coach wanted to change signals to make the team better.

Shared by Braden Boss

Helping Athletes Buy into the Philosophy that Mistakes are Part of Learning

Here are additional ideas for how coaches can reinforce the team philosophy that mistakes are part of learning:

- **Discuss the "Mistakes are Part of Learning" philosophy with athletes**. Coaches can lead discussions with their athletes to help them understand the team's approach to dealing with mistakes as learning opportunities. They need to talk through this concept with athletes to give them a chance to think about what it means to take this approach and what it looks like day to day on their teams. This gives athletes a chance to ask questions, share their views, and wrap their heads around this approach. Coaches can revisit the concept often with individual athletes as well as the entire team. A coach could start the discussion with something like this:

> *"I really believe that if we can approach mistakes as part of learning this season it will be a key to our success. I've watched athletes become so discouraged and dejected after making mistakes, and that can lead to making more mistakes. I think it would be amazing if we could all embrace this idea that we know mistakes make us better. We know we will make mistakes and that we are resilient and can overcome them. We know we can play a big role in helping one another adopt this philosophy. Too many teams are taken down by their mistakes. Someone makes a mistake that leads to them making more mistakes. Mistakes can be contagious, so that they spread across the entire team. I want us to be a team that is like Lieutenant Dan in Forrest Gump. Remember that scene where he climbs the ship pole in that terrible storm and is yelling? That's how I see us, we're on that pole, telling mistakes to come our way because we will learn from them and overcome them. They will not take us down."*

  Whatever the examples and whatever the strategies, coaches have to help athletes completely buy into the "Mistakes are Part of Learning" philosophy.

- **Help athletes develop the skill of responding positively to their teammates after mistakes.** Athletes have to not only buy in to the "Mistakes are part of learning" philosophy, but coaches also have to help athletes develop the skill to respond in effective ways when their teammates make mistakes. They have to provide support in a positive and caring manner to their teammates. They have to realize that everyone on the team will make mistakes across the season, and the way in which teammates respond to mistakes is huge. Sometimes athletes call each other out (for example, on social media, in the weight room, on the field) in ways that they may perceive (and coaches often encourage) as providing leadership but in reality may be harmful. So often the athletes that do more calling out of others are the ones that desire to be positive leaders but may need guidance.

- **Encourage athletes to be problem solvers.** Instead of getting upset when athletes make mistakes, coaches can help their athletes figure out how the team can respond to errors and make improvements. A great example of this is described by Braden in Climate in Action 5.4, who is remembering a baseball coach he had as an adolescent. We have observed many baseball coaches get upset when athletes misread signals for bunting, stealing, hit and run plays, etc. It is not unusual for athletes to be punished with running/physical conditioning and harsh words from the coach. Braden describes how his coach used a missed signal to take time for the team to discuss how the signals could be improved.

CLIMATE IN ACTION 5.5

Pete Carroll (Coach of the Seattle Seahawks) and Bruce Arians (Coach of the Arizona Cardinals) had very different responses to their field goal kickers when they missed relatively easy kicks (less than 30 yards) to win the game for their teams in a 2016 NFL playoff game.[3]

Pete Carroll said this about his athlete: "*[Hauschka] made his kicks to give us a chance and unfortunately he didn't make the last one. He's been making kicks for years around here … but he's gonna hit a lot of winners as we go down the road here. I love him and he's our guy.*"

When Bruce Arians was asked what words he had for his athlete, the tone and message was quite different: "*Make it. He's a professional. This ain't high school. You get paid to make it.*"

While Arians' words are true, his athlete gets paid well to make these kinds of kicks, the truth is that these talented professional athletes make mistakes, and which athlete is going to be more likely to bounce back from this mistake and come through in the clutch in the future? How nice that Hauschka has a coach recognizing his disappointment that he wasn't able to come through for the team, but being quick to notice how many times he has performed at a high level and served the team well. How important to hear Carroll's words to remind him that he is loved, he's important and valued on the team, and one mistake doesn't change any of that.

- **Track the team's comebacks**. Coaches should keep track of the comebacks their team has had, the best innings, the best string of points the team has put together, the most points the team has ever scored in a quarter or a half, etc. This can occur both within single competitions but also across the season. For example, one season a team lost eight games in a row but then won the last 10 games of the season. Something we notice in our work with young athletes, in general, is that many of them give up quickly and rapidly develop a "*We are going to lose*" mentality. There often is not a, "*Hey they had a good inning; now it's our turn*" mentality, or a spirit of "*This season is not over yet.*" One of the great lessons athletes can learn is the ability to think positively and give their best effort through every game and every season. One strategy coaches can use to help athletes develop this strong sense of perseverance is to note every comeback the team has and to actually track those and discuss them with their athletes. Comebacks occur every week in sport at every level, so it is crazy that any team would ever give up. Not only can coaches talk about their own team's ability to bounce back, but also frequently share examples of others' comebacks. One of our favorites is Billy Mills' come from behind victory to win the gold medal in the 10,000 meter race in the 1964 Tokyo Olympics. Another is the Colts comeback against the Patriots in the NFL AFC Championship game in 2007. The Patriots, one of the best NFL teams of the last 15 years, lead 21–3 at the half, and the Colts made a strong comeback in the 2nd half to win the game. They also went on to win the Super Bowl that year. Coaches can do an online search for great comebacks and come up with a number of examples for any sport. When coaches have frequent discussions about never giving up and rebounding after mistakes, it sets a tone for athletes to focus on being the best they can be, and understanding that mistakes will happen all along the way.

- **Teach athletes that one player <u>never</u> is the reason for a loss.** Another strategy that is key for coaches is to help athletes see that one player never loses a game. It is easy for athletes to focus on the last play or plays of the game, and think that whoever struck-out with runners on base, fumbled in the last minutes of the game, or had a turnover was probably to blame for the loss. However, this is rarely the case when coaches lay out the entire game. That is, looking back there were many plays where athletes could have made tackles, gotten hits, scored points, and overall had opportunities to help the team advance. The point is that losses are all about teams and the overall performance and never about a single athlete's mistake. Athletes need to be part of discussions where coaches reinforce these points so they do not get caught catastrophizing over a single play.

- **Mistakes are part of life.** We all make them and some of our mistakes are bigger and more public than others. It is important for athletes to have coaches that can use both the smaller and bigger mistakes as teachable moments. Often we read of events that happen in sport where an athlete engages in egregious behavior (flagrant fouls on the court that endanger athletes, are arrested for assault). In a caring and task-involving climate, coaches are trying to provide support and guidance to athletes, even when the mistakes they have made are significant, public, embarrassing to the team and the program, and/or go against every core value the coach, team, program may hold. Sometimes athletes who engage in these behaviors are shunned from the team, banned from campus, etc. We appreciate when coaches strive to use mistakes like these as powerful and valuable teachable moments. Coaches can speak with athletes about the mistakes they make and how these incidents do not need to define them. Coaches can encourage athletes to apologize to all involved and commit to being a better athlete and person in the future. How tremendous it would be if athletes learn from these experiences, by having coaches that truly support them in dark moments of their lives. Most people really value having those few individuals in their lives who provide unconditional love and support, and note how powerful it can be if coaches and teammates are those kinds of individuals. Certainly, the coach, team, and the administration are justifiably frustrated when poor images are cast on their schools, but care needs to be taken to help athletes learn and grow from their mistakes (see Climate in Action 5.5).

- **Doers make mistakes.** Perhaps former UCLA basketball coach and genius, John Wooden, said it best: "If you're not making mistakes, then you're not doing anything. I'm positive that a doer makes mistakes."[4] Coaches should be highlighting examples for their athletes of how much expertise directly results from learning from mistakes. Recently, we were complimenting a friend, Susumu, who had made a delicious dinner for us, and lamenting that we do not have the ability to prepare amazing food in the way he does. Our friend laughed and said he learned from the many mistakes he made along the way. He figured out what temperatures and times to cook, what combination of spices worked best, etc. the hard way as he had many disasters and unfortunate outcomes along the way. It is easy to see people who demonstrate incredible abilities and skills (e.g., piano, vocal performance, fashion, literary) that we would love to possess, and think that they were just imbued with these attributes, forgetting how much time went into developing these strengths.

- **Consider mistakes in practice versus competition.** Athletes and coaches can feel like mistakes in practice are much easier to stomach than in competition. However, if coaches buy in to the "Mistakes are Part of Learning" approach, it has to encompass both practice and competition. The disappointment and investment may be greater in competition, but the bottom line is that whatever the situation, the response is to stay focused on learning from what happened today and getting better tomorrow. This is what individuals have to do in their jobs, and in their roles as parents, partners, and friends. Life is about making the most of today, applying what we learned, and being a little bit better tomorrow.

- **Share powerful quotes often.** Coaches can look for ways to share quotes on a frequent basis that reinforce the philosophy that overcoming mistakes and struggles are part of what gives life purpose and meaning. Fred Rogers, the children's television show host, said, "*The people who struggle the most in life are the ones who inspire me the most.*"[5] John Maxwell said, "*In life, the question is not if you will have problems, but how you are going to deal with your problems. If the possibility of failure were erased, what would you attempt to achieve?*"[6] Kevin Olson, a talented high school athlete who made one poor split-second decision in life (jumped in a lake not realizing how shallow the water was) has had to come to terms with the consequence of living the rest of his life with paralysis.[7] In his book, *Learning to Live with It*, he writes, "I began to ask myself, 'Am I going to allow my problems to defeat me, or to develop me?'

Am I going to allow the unwanted events in my life to make me bitter, or use them to make me better?'" If athletes like Kevin can give life their best in these circumstances, how much easier should it be for athletes that face much less significant obstacles. Quotes like these can serve as reminders to athletes that their struggles are not without purpose. Coaches can use these quotes as discussion starters before or after practice, or during warmups or cooldowns to expand on these ideas. Coaches might even think about having older athletes lead the discussion.

- **Keep the eye on the development prize.** While most youth sport coaches know that development should be the driving force within youth sport, and all young athletes should have opportunities to play and enhance their skills and knowledge of the game, it is easy for coaches, in the heat of a competition, to shift the focus to only winning. It is helpful to be reminded that even at the professional level many coaches struggle with this concept. That is why it is interesting to see quotes like this one from Ned Yost, the manager of the World Champion Kansas City Royals who said,[8]

> "*I wanted to put those young players in a position to gain experience, so that when we could compete for a championship, they'd know how,*" Yost says. "*You can't do that when you're pinch-hitting for young guys. You can't do it when you quick-hook starting pitchers. They'll never learn to work themselves out of trouble. People would say, 'What's he doing?' They didn't understand. I'd rather lose a game on my watch so they could win later.*"

If this is true at the professional level, how much more relevant is it at the youth sport level? Young athletes need to have opportunities to play in competitions where they can make mistakes and learn from them. So often coaches put young athletes into a game for a minute, but as Ned Yost suggests, they "quick-hook" them if they make a dribbling or passing error. These athletes can find themselves right back on the bench. They have not even had time for their heart rates to come down or to settle into the game. Boom, they are in and out of the game already. This happens while other athletes may get the benefit of the doubt and have the luxury of playing an entire quarter or half. They have a chance to go up and down the field or court a few times and make adjustments. When athletes get pulled so quickly, it can hinder their confidence and learning opportunities. It would be great if more youth sport coaches were like Ned Yost, and allowed their athletes a chance to experience the game, and along the way were reassuring their athletes to cut themselves slack, to not worry about every mistake, and to just let themselves get used to the game.

Strategies coaches can use on this front is to have a plan going into the game for playing time, thinking through how the coach plans to get athletes into the game. Coaches might also have a saying on a clipboard or get a tattoo (just kidding) with words that serve to trigger their preferred coaching responses (mistakes are part of learning; be a doer; no fear).

- **Create drills to help athletes who are hesitant to make mistakes**. So often we watch youth sport practices and there is an athlete or two who have no hesitation, for example, taking shots, while another couple of athletes **NEVER** shoot. The coach might encourage the non-shooters to be shooters, and the athletes might nod in agreement that they will take shots, but they do not. This hurts the team because a few athletes learn to have no fear and shoot all the time and others do not develop in this area. One strategy a coach could try is to set up a drill where only the non-shooting athletes can take shots. This means that the typical shooters have to work hard to set the non-shooters up for shots. Clearly the coach would not do this drill for an hour of practice, but even doing it 5–10 minutes would allow time for the team to understand the value of others shooting. Regardless of the outcomes of the shots (whether the non-shooters make their shots), it is the first step in helping these athletes gain confidence to take shots and understanding how this helps the team (*"When an opponent double teams Quinn/Honey during a game we need you to take the shots."*). Quinn and Honey may need a lot of encouragement and how exciting when their shots start to fall. The coach can lead discussion with the team that could look something like this:

> *"I wanted us to work on this drill because we are not fully capitalizing on the talents of Beth and Ollie right now. They are more likely to let Quinn and Honey shoot. This is kind of a big deal because we can't be the team we want to be without everyone getting confident taking shots. We have to take a good number of shots to get comfortable even being willing to throw the ball up, so that was our goal in that drill. I want us supporting and encouraging Beth and Ollie to shoot both in practice and in games. Does everyone get why this is so important?"*

This kind of discussion brings the athletes in and helps them understand that the coach is not just calling out Beth and Ollie; rather, the coach wants all athletes to develop confidence in contributing to the team.

- **Take the "Mistakes are Part of Learning" philosophy to weight rooms.** One area where the "mistakes are part of learning" approach could be transformational occurs in weight rooms across middle and high schools. We have heard many athletes describe how they and/or their teammates have bad experiences in strength training programs where ego-involving climates prevail. Weight rooms definitely are places where athletes' physical strength and prowess (or lack of such), can be on display for all to see. During the middle and high school years, young athletes are experiencing considerable physical changes and for those who have poor technique, little experience, and who may be physically less mature, weight rooms can pose frustrating and sometimes humiliating circumstances. Athletes describe how some coaches are unaware of how much teasing goes on in weight rooms, so it is very important that coaches are intentional about creating a training space where athletes are reassured and encouraged to move at their own pace, to support one another, to understand that the goal is for everyone to develop great technique, to strive to improve each day, and above all, to understand that mistakes are part of the learning process. If coaches can create this environment in strength training areas, it would be beneficial for all athletes, and especially those who are vulnerable in various ways (e.g., less confident, lower skilled, have small physical stature). More experienced and mature athletes can help coaches infuse this philosophy throughout a training program.

- **Look closely at all forms of punishment used with athletes.** Another way coaches can instill the "mistakes are part of learning" approach is to think very carefully about how and when they use punishment. We often observe coaches using running for punishment in ways that they feel may be motivating, but when taking a closer look are definitely counter-productive. For example, one volleyball coach ended practice with a drill where all the athletes in the program (11–18-year-olds) lined up on the baseline of the gym. When the whistle was blown, athletes had to run to the end of the gym and back, and whoever placed first was rewarded with permission to leave practice, while the remaining athletes continued to run the laps. This took place for another 30 laps until only one athlete remained. The coach clearly was not thinking, "How can I end practice in such a way as to completely kill all excitement and enthusiasm on the team?" Even so, that was the result, and this wrap-up to practice was a disaster on many fronts. This example highlights how coaches need to think carefully about how the activities they choose for their athletes can generate excitement, enjoyment, teamwork or just as easily kill these important outcomes. Athletes' competence, commitment, and feelings of team comradery can take a hit when they are on the receiving end of punishment. That said, conditioning is important. Coaches can inspire athletes to work hard, get in great shape, and not be in a vulnerable position due to their lack of conditioning, but the approach described above is not helpful for achieving these goals.

- **Coaches can imagine how they want to respond during stressful times.** An important strategy coaches can use is to visualize the role model they want to be for their athletes in stressful times. Sometimes coaches show their frustration quickly (i.e., display negative body language, withdrawal from active coaching, become overly critical or pessimistic) when a team is struggling, and they may not realize the impact their behavior has on athletes. A beneficial exercise for coaches is to think through the intentional behavior they want to engage in when the team is in stressful periods. When coaches think about it, they likely want to provide encouraging words, display positive body language, and feel high confidence; they want their athletes to do the same. A fun exercise to do might be creating "if-then" cue cards. If an athlete makes a mental mistake, the coach would prefer to [engage in this behavior]. If an athlete is playing scared, the coach would prefer to [engage in this behavior]. If an athlete is demonstrating poor technique, a coach would prefer to [engage in this behavior]. These cards could remind coaches to strive to bring enthusiasm and energy to these situations and to build confidence within athletes. For example, Lora coaches a middle school basketball team. Her team has been working on offensive plays in practice. In the next game, the team executes a play poorly, and she has this "response to mistakes" ready: "*I first take a deep breath (inhaling and exhaling fully) … and tell myself, 'I believe in my team' before responding. This serves to keep me positive (in words and body language) so that I come back to my team in a way that will be productive.*"

- **Develop mistake rituals for the team.** A wonderful way to guide athletes in helping their teammates deal with mistakes in a positive manner is to create Mistake Rituals for athletes and for teams, a strategy endorsed by the Positive Coaching Alliance.[9] For example, football coach Joe Claunch helped his team develop a mistake ritual. They decided to reach back and touch their shoulder when someone on the team made a mistake as a symbol that every player on the team has that athlete's back. How cool for athletes to have this symbol (to touch the back) to be reminded that their team is with them all the way. Coaches can have athletes brainstorm rituals that the team or individual athletes might use. Sport psychology consultant Ken Ravizza helped the California State University, Fullerton baseball team adopt a mistake ritual.[10] The team kept a miniature toilet in their dugout to remind athletes to flush mistakes (made a bad throw; swung at a ball outside the strike-zone) when they occurred. Sometimes athletes have a difficult time letting mistakes go. They may be thinking they have let their teammates down, so what a great ritual to have to remind athletes after mistakes that everyone is a member of a united team that leaves mistakes behind to focus on the next play.
- **Try on a little empathy.** Some coaches may find it taxing to work with athletes who have low skill levels that lead to frequent mistakes, particularly if the coaches are or were skilled athletes. One tip coaches might try in this situation is to think about an activity where they have low skills. For example, some coaches might be uncomfortable on the dance floor, playing tennis, or performing a squat in weight lifting. They might also think of activities where they are highly skilled and try doing those with their non-dominant limbs (e.g., throwing with non-dominant hand). In this case, coaches might be reminded of how these activities do not come naturally or easy for them, and it could lead them to have greater empathy for their athletes who are making mistakes and who need more time to develop.
- **Treat athletes well every day.** One thing we find unfortunate is when athletes tell us that coaches treat them much better when they are playing well than when they have poor performances. Athletes describe how some

coaches talk to their athletes more, make more eye contact, show greater interest in them, and make them feel valued and connected to the team when these athletes have strong performances. It makes athletes feel like their coaches do not really care about them; rather, they only care about winning, and if athletes are not directly contributing at the moment to the team's success on the scoreboard, coaches sometimes have less interest in them. What is odd about this scenario is that athletes are in greater need of their coaches' positive attention when they have an off day or are in a rut, yet many athletes describe how they only receive positive attention (eye contact, greeting, etc.) from their coach on the good performance days. When it comes to adopting the view that mistakes are part of learning, coaches need to be sure they are reinforcing their support of athletes each day, regardless of their performance. A reminder is that coaches are coaching people, and not performances. As Pete Carroll, the Seattle Seahawks NFL coach, says, "*People make mistakes all the time. We learn and grow. If there's patience and love, and you care for people, you can work them through it, and they can find their greatest heights.*"[11]

When is Punishment Appropriate to Use?

As we wrap up this chapter, some readers may be asking the question, "So is punishment ever okay to use?" Our answer to this question is yes, there are times when punishment is appropriate. However, we would encourage coaches to think about these points before proceeding to use punishment with their teams:

- Punishment should be used sparingly.
- Before coaches use punishment, they should talk with athletes to get their perspective and to understand what might be going on behind the scenes (see Correcting Behavioral Issues in Chapter 10).
- Punishment should only be used in situations where athletes have control over the situation (for example, when an athlete acted in a disrespectful manner to an opposing player or coach).
- Punishment should be delivered in a caring manner where athletes understand that their coach is trying to help them, and wants them to learn from their mistakes (see Discipline with Care in Chapter 3).
- Coaches should avoid using physical activity as punishment, as considerable research has shown this approach to be counterproductive for short and long-term athlete motivation.
- Coaches, together with their athletes, should establish expectations for the team's behavior at the beginning of the season so that all can understand the importance of making a commitment to honor the guidelines for the team.

We would urge youth sport coaches to think carefully about how and under what circumstances they use punishment, because the truth is that many coaches may not need to use punishment across an entire season. In this chapter, we cannot do justice to the topic of when punishment is appropriate to use because there are so many aspects to consider such as the particular offense, the age of the athletes, the level of the sport, etc. We suggest that punishment is one of the more important topics coaches can think about and that can impact their effectiveness. Lastly, regardless of the offense an athlete may have committed, our mantra in this chapter is to remind coaches that regardless of the reason (mental, physical, lack of knowledge) mistakes are made, they should be considered avenues for learning, growing, and developing as athletes and people.

*****

One of the greatest lessons that athletes can take from sport is the idea that mistakes are part of learning. How fortunate athletes are when they have coaches that help them learn this lesson as it applies to sport as well as life. This chapter provides food for thought for coaches who are trying to instill this philosophy with their athletes. It may be one of the most challenging but important successes coaches can have with their teams. If athletes can gain the view that life is filled with mistakes, and learning from mistakes is a key to success, then they will be on their way to have meaningful experiences.

Reflecting on Practice

Responding to Mistakes: Observing My Coaching Responses

Sometimes coaches find it very helpful to take a few moments to reflect on their own and the athletes' responses when punishment versus positive and energized encouragement is used in practices and games. This activity is for the purpose of contrasting reactions to your different coaching behaviors. For coaches who come from a sport tradition where punishment is used frequently, it might be helpful to experiment or pay closer attention to the reaction that you and your athletes have when you respond negatively with punishment in comparison to positive reinforcement. It might also be an interesting team discussion to have with athletes, and to hear their perspective on how they respond to both the coaches and their teammates' punishing vs. supportive behaviors.

- Notice when you catch yourself being positive, encouraging and offering genuine feedback to athletes after mistakes. How does this affect your energy, your focus, and your enjoyment of the practice/game?
- How do positive words, encouragement, and genuine feedback affect your athletes? How does this affect their energy, their focus, and their enjoyment of the practice/game? How do different athletes respond?
- Notice when you catch yourself going negative and using punishment with your athletes. What is your response? How does this affect your energy, your focus, and your enjoyment of the practice/game?
- How does punishment affect your athletes? How does this affect their energy, their focus, and their enjoyment of the practice/game? How do different athletes respond?
- How do your responses vary based on whether you are interacting with a more or less skilled athlete? Is your response to them making a mistake different, and if so how?
- Which athletes on your team could benefit most from ideas in this chapter? How so?
- What areas of embracing the "Mistakes are Part of Learning" philosophy that were highlighted in this chapter could you add based on your observations of your current coaching practice?

Communities of Practice

- Read this chapter with a coach friend (or your coaching staff) and discuss how it could be relevant for your team.
- Try logging/journaling your efforts to emphasize mistakes are part of learning. Describe the strategies you use in practice/competition and the effect they have on you and your athletes.

Sources

[1] Claunch, J. & Fry, M. D. (2016). Native American football coaches' experience of a motivational climate collaboration with sport psychology researchers. *International Journal of Sports Science & Coaching*, 11, 482–495.

[2] Wilson, M. A., Cushion, C. J., & Stephens, D. E. (2006). Put me in coach! I'm better than you think I am: Coaches' perceptions of their expectations in youth sport. *International Journal of Sports Science and Coaching*, 1 , 149–161.

[3] Bien, L. (2016). Pete Carroll and Bruce Arians had very different reactions to their kickers missing chip shot field goals: I know which of these head coaches I'd rather have as my dad. Retrieved April 20, 2019 from SB Nation: www.sbnation.com/2016/10/24/13378128/cardinals-seahawks-missed-field-goals-overtime-sunday-night

[4] Wooden, J. Retrieved April 20, 2019: www.thewoodeneffect.com/motivational-quotes/

[5] Quote for Mr. Rogers. (2018). *Won't You Be My Neighbor?* – IMDb

[6] Maxwell, J. C. (2000). *Failing forward: Turning mistakes into stepping-stones for success.* Nashville, TN: Thomas Nelson.

[7] Olson, K. (2013). *Learning to live with it.* USA: Xulon. [pp.80–81].

[8] Schoenfeld, B. (2015, October 1). How Ned Yost made the Kansas City Royals unstoppable. New York Times. Retrieved April 20, 2019: www.nytimes.com/2015/10/04/magazine/how-ned-yost-made-the-kansas-city-royals-unstoppable.html

[9] Positive Coaching Alliance. *Developing mistake rituals.* Retrieved April 19, 2019 from the PCA Development Zone Resource Center: https://devzone.positivecoach.org/resource/worksheet/developing-mistake-ritual

[10] Ravizza, K. & Hanson, T. (1995). *Heads up baseball.* Chicago, IL: McGraw-Hill

[11] Carroll, P. Retrieved from AZ Quotes April 20, 2019: www.azquotes.com/quote/1215575

6

FEATURES OF A CARING AND TASK-INVOLVING CLIMATE IN SPORT

Every Athlete Plays an Important Role on the Team

Highlights

- Athletes are very aware of the quality and quantity of feedback their coaches give them.
- Coaches can be intentional in helping all athletes see the valuable contributions they make to the team.
- Many strategies are provided that coaches can consider using to make all their athletes feel they play an important role on the team.

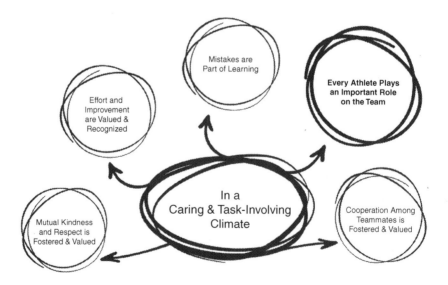

Every athlete is considered to be an equally important member of the team in a caring and task-involving climate. On some teams there is a strong sense that a few athletes are the most important members. These athletes typically score more points, have the highest ability and performance, and often receive more recognition (are mentioned by name or pictured in a newspaper article). In a caring and task-involving climate, coaches are trying to instill the philosophy that there is no hierarchy among athletes. Of course athletes bring different qualities, attributes, and skill levels to the team, but the point is that a team never reaches its potential until the important contribution of all members of the team is recognized and fulfilled. In this chapter, we provide strategies to help coaches think about what they are doing to help every athlete realize the important contribution they make to the team and to help the team embrace the philosophy that none are above others.

Identifying and Communicating the Important Contributions that Each Athlete Makes to the Team

- **Call athletes by name.** One way that coaches convey that every team member is important is by calling athletes by their preferred name. It is such a basic thing that it seems unnecessary to even mention, but calling athletes by name is a crucial first step. Many athletes describe how they are unsure of whether their coach knows them by name, and even if coaches know their athletes' names, it is helpful for coaches to do a self-check and pay attention to how often they are using their athletes' names when they speak to them. Referring to athletes using their surnames does not allow for the same personal connection to occur as when coaches call athletes by their first names, and calling some athletes by name and not others sends a direct message about who is most valued. Finally, athletes appreciate when coaches make the effort to call them by their preferred names ("Bo" rather than Beauregard) as it makes them feel more comfortable.
- **Talk to athletes.** It would be easy to make the assumption that coaches are talking directly with their athletes at each practice and competition, but many athletes report having coaches that do not interact with them in a personal way for significant lengths of time (even days). The coach may be addressing the team overall, but fail to make eye contact and talk directly to some athletes. If coaches are having conversations with a few athletes, but not all, it can definitely result in some athletes not feeling as valued as others. Here are a few ideas on this front:
  - o **Greet athletes every day.** Coaches should greet each athlete as they arrive at practices and competition, and encourage athletes to greet one another. If some athletes receive greetings but not others, it can be seen as a direct message to all about who is most valued on the team, and if no personal greetings are given, it is an energy drainer on the team.

o **Have a conversation with each athlete each week**. Coaches can do a self-check and think back about what kind of exchange they have had with their athletes each day and each week. One athlete told us that his coach did not speak directly to him the first several months he was on the team. It was not until a few months in that the coach began talking to him. This athlete observed that the coach was definitely having conversations with athletes, he just was not one of them, and it made the athlete feel like he was not an important athlete on the team. When coaches refer even to little things like, "*How was your day, Sam?*" or "*What did you think about that drill, Hannah?*", it radars to athletes that the coach is seeing them, and desiring to include them. Without these direct interactions, athletes can be unsure of their connection to the coach and the team. We often have young athletes tell us that their coaches do not like them, and when we ask why, their response is often something like this, "*I don't know. I can just tell. He/she never smiles and doesn't think I'm any good.*" We are suggesting that while it seems small, when coaches are intentional about interacting with their athletes, it is a pretty big deal.

• **Give all athletes high quantity and quality of feedback.** One aspect of coaching behaviors that can vary dramatically among athletes is the amount and quality of feedback that they receive from their coaches. It is not unusual for the more talented and skilled athletes on a team to receive more feedback from coaches. Although this seems counterintuitive (because less skilled athletes need more feedback), coaches are sometimes focused on helping their best athletes improve because it may be seen as having a more direct impact on the team's immediate performance. However, coaches who create a caring and task-involving climate on their teams strive to give every athlete high quality feedback often. Here are examples ...

o **Example 1**
  • "*Matt, good job.*" Feedback like this is considered to be general and vague. While it is okay to use this type of feedback sometimes, it is easy to overuse it. The problem is that it is not necessarily clear what was good.
  • "*Tina, good job. You are really keeping your head still on that swing as you hit the golf ball. I can tell a huge difference in how you are consistently keeping your head stable on both the back swing and the forward swing. Can you see your improvement on this?*" Notice how the feedback is much more directed for Tina than it is for Matt. Tina is not left with a question about the source of the compliment.
o **Example 2**
  • "*Sidney, stay consistent with your serving motion on your first and second serve.*"

- *"Tea, I'm noticing on your first serve that you are doing a nice job getting that knee bend, tossing arm stretched high after the release, and good contact point and follow-through. On your second serve, it seems like you are wanting to play it a little safer and it is resulting in you losing that good form. You aren't bending the knees as much, your tossing arm is releasing the ball, and then you're dropping that hand too quickly, resulting in your head and body dropping. When this happens, it's easy to hit the serve into the net. What do you think? [athlete agrees]. Okay, so really work on keeping that same nice technique on your second serve at practice today. Don't worry about double faulting for now. The important thing is to keep bending your knees, stretching that toss hand high and leaving it up after the release, so that you can have that natural follow-through."*

With this example, Tea is getting in-depth, high quality feedback. The coach is helping Tea understand the specifics of what is happening to his service motion on his second serve. The coach is demonstrating for him, whereas with Sidney, the coach is not describing what this consistency entails. Some coaches might assume that Sidney may know what it means to be consistent but if the coach has not explained it previously, she probably will not perceive the feedback as helpful.

Research has revealed that coaches give more and better feedback to high skilled athletes, but coaches who are creating a caring and task-involving climate are committed to giving every athlete on their team high quantity and quality of feedback.[1] While this is tough to do, it is a huge part of helping all athletes feel they are important members of the team. Athletes have lamented to us that their coaches would send them to the other end of the gym to shoot around a while or work on something, while the coaches worked with the best athletes. This might be okay if the coach switched at some point and gave the other athletes feedback, but sometimes this does not happen and it contributes to athletes feeling that they are less valued and important to the team.

CLIMATE IN ACTION 6.1

In a research study by Becker and Wrisberg in which they closely examined the winningest women's basketball coach in history, Pat Summitt, they found that during practice her coaching behaviors were split between the team (54%) and individual athletes (46%). Most interesting in their findings was that there was no difference in either the quality or quantity of her coaching behaviors with her higher and lower skilled athletes. One of the features that made Coach Summitt a great coach was her ability to treat every athlete as an important member of her team.

In Climate in Action 6.2, Coach Jessica Smith describes how she helps her athletes who currently make up the scouting squad (are not starters) fully understand the key role they play in helping the team reach its potential. She talks to athletes about the important role they play and helps them embrace it as they strive to further develop and become a starter.

CLIMATE IN ACTION 6.2

Everyone plays a role on the team and each woman must play her role to the best of her ability, with the good of the team always at the forefront of actions and efforts made. However, not everyone is going to get the playing time they want and that can be really tough with the commitment and sacrifices that must be made at the Division I level. I am convinced that the team will not win if every single player on the squad doesn't view their role as important. For example, the players who consistently play on the scout group and don't get many game minutes, are the players who are creating the training environment for the core group. If the scout group doesn't believe in their role, their ability to challenge the core group and their ability to break into the core group, then the training environment will not prepare the team to be competitive in matches. Therefore, the scout group MUST know and believe their value and that starts from the coaching staff, but becomes the culture of the team. Instead of telling the scout team to play a formation and wait to be rotated in, I paint a detailed picture of what the team needs from them. I explain each positional role and I coach it during their time on the field. I praise them for execution and I demand a high standard they must meet, which shows them what they are doing matters. Consequently, the team is energized to compete, instead of waiting for their turn on the core group.

Shared by Jessica Smith (Associate Head Volleyball Coach, Kansas State University)

- **Highlight athletes' many and varied contributions to the team.** Just like parents have children with very different personalities, gifts, and attributes, the same is true for coaches and their athletes. Coaches can do much to help athletes see in themselves (and help others see in their teammates) the things they do that really contribute to the team. Here are some examples of how coaches can note these special behaviors that are key to making the team better:
  - o **Examples for individual athletes**
    - *"Eujean, I appreciate how you show up at practice both mentally and physically ready. You are always on time, have all your gear, you are focused and are*

ready to step on the field and get zoned in. I love how you are consistently here and ready to go using all cylinders."

- *"Zeno, I notice how you support and encourage Dale and Martin. They have been a little discouraged about their performance at the plate, and it really helps having teammates that keep believing in you and providing encouragement."*
- *"Carolyn, I want to thank you for your extra high effort in that fast break drill today. It's tough to work on that at the end of practice but we needed to, and it felt like your determination helped the team rally and get the most out of that drill."*
- *"Dimitrije, I feel like you really support Coach Reedy and me, and I just wanted you to know that we notice it and we appreciate it. Coaching is hard and it means a lot when you have supportive athletes."*
- *"I want to give a shout out to Vera after today's match. She lost the first set 6-0, but she refocused and started fresh in the second set and came on with gusto. She was facing a strong opponent and it would have been easy to not fight as hard as she could to get back in the match, but she sure didn't give it up. Vera, nice job displaying determination today."*

In talking with the team, a coach might refer to Babe Didrickson Zaharias, and then ask the team who that is. The coach knows that Sheryl is likely to be able to tell the team that, *"She was one of the greatest female athletes of all time. She won two Olympic medals in track, and played golf professionally."* The coach could respond with something as simple as, *"Yes, and it's fun and important for us to know about great athletes who have come before us."* This acknowledges Sheryl's interest in the history of the game as being a valuable contribution to the team.

CLIMATE IN ACTION 6.3

A swim coach takes the team values (e.g., discipline, passion, mindfulness, work ethic) and develops a word of the week. Throughout the week, athletes are then encouraged to identify other members of the team who represent the word of the week (e.g., strong work ethic) and record what they observed and place it in a box (e.g., *"I saw how Gwynn really worked hard and maintained her goal time on our set of 10 x 100's today – Go Gwynn!"*). At the end of the week, the coach reads out the observations to all of the swimmers and then highlights other examples she has noticed throughout the week (e.g., *"Thanks for sharing all of your examples! I also want to give a shout out to Kelly for coming in before practice on Thursday to work on her starts and turns for the meet tomorrow. I appreciated her putting in the extra time and effort to improve her swimming times. Great work!"*).

o **Examples for groups of athletes within the team.** Coaches can also help their teams by noticing great behaviors by sub-groups within the team such as starters, non-starters, offense, defense, seniors, rookies, etc. Here are some examples:

- After a win, a coach might say, "*Gals, I think we need to recognize the amazing contribution our bench made to this win tonight. They brought such energy and support to the team, and it's pretty awesome to have athletes who get how important their role is and really embrace that role. Let's all tip our hat to our bench tonight. Awesome job, Amelie, Sarah, Ella, Jennifer, and Jordan.*"

- After a loss against a strong opponent, a coach might say, "*Guys, I love how hard we fought in this game. It makes me proud to be your coach, and to see that commitment to giving our best. I want to say to our players who didn't get much playing time tonight, that our strong performance tonight had a lot to do with how you worked hard in practice this week to help the team prepare. The high quality of our practices impacted the way in which we were able to play this team so close (closer, in fact, than we've played them in several years) and your hard work definitely does not go unnoticed.*"

- A coach tells his senior (or older athletes), "*I want you to know that your leadership on this team is powerful in many ways. You are doing such a great job and helping the younger players feel valued and connected. These younger athletes are the future of the Bears soccer team, and they will be so much better because of the way you are helping them develop and believe in themselves. Not every team is fortunate to have a group that gets the important role they play like you athletes seem to understand. What a difference it makes. Thank you, Asher, Asa, Xavier, Janek, & Jack.*"

- In a discussion with athletes who do not currently get much playing time a coach might say, "*I know all of you would like to get more playing time. I want to encourage you to keep working hard, and to just know that I'm trying to do all I can to help each of you continue to develop. I also want to remind you that things can change quickly, where an athlete might have to be taken out of the lineup because of an injury or family situation, so we need everyone to be ready to play. Above all, I hope you realize how much your effort contributes to the team. You are making our starters better everyday, and you are going to appreciate that about your teammates when you move into that starting role.*"

These are a few examples that highlight small things coaches can say and share with their athletes that might have helpful ripple effects. That is, sometimes coaches may be thinking these things, but not verbalizing them, and it is important for all athletes to receive these kinds of kudos from coaches. When athletes receive this feedback, it is a way of helping them see the value of sharing these compliments, and may help them develop the skill to notice these things in others and pass them on. This is where the ripples are initiated.

- **Help every athlete develop their assistant coach skills.** Coaches can heighten their athletes' engagement in the team, and their sense of feeling valued by including athletes in assessment and decision making related to the team. While some coaches have a "My way or the highway philosophy" (I have all the answers for this team), a much more useful approach is helping athletes understand that they have much to contribute to making the team better. Here are some activities that may give coaches ideas for how they could empower their athletes to notice and share their thoughts to make their teammates and the team better.

  o **Teach athletes on the bench.** Often, athletes who are sitting on the bench are removed from the coaching staff, and their levels of involvement in the game can vary. This can be a missed opportunity so coaches might try spacing themselves out on the bench so athletes can be on either side of them all the way down the bench. This strategic seating arrangement may provide a wonderful chance for coaches to point out what athletes and opponents are doing well, and how they could improve. Specifically, coaches can highlight technique, strategy, knowledge of the rules, and other aspects of the sport. They can ask athletes to notice things athletes are doing well, and areas that they are striving to improve. Besides providing an opportunity for athletes to interact with coaches during games when possible, coaches can also get athletes' input at the end of a game or at the end of practice. In team discussions, coaches can ask questions like, "*What did we do well today in practice?*"; "*What do we need to keep working hard to improve?*"; or "*What are the top three things we did well in our match today?*" Too often the coach is doing all the summarizing, identifying all the take home points, and deciding on the next steps for the team. When this is the case, it is easy for some athletes to tune out and not be listening closely. Clearly, it is fun for a team to hear different voices and perspectives.

  o **Providing avenues for athletes to make suggestions for the good of the team.** Some coaches might not think about the value of encouraging their athletes to make suggestions about the teams. This is too bad because it results in a lack of utilizing young people's creative and clever minds, and prevents them from developing important skills associated with critical thinking and leadership. Young athletes can have great ideas that could benefit the team. Of course, just because the coach receives suggestions from athletes does not mean he/she would act on every suggestion. It does, however, mean that coaches are acknowledging that they do not know everything, and they are aware that their athletes are sharp young people, capable of helping the team become the best it can be. Coaches could welcome athletes' suggestions for drills, practice schedules, team building activities, and really for everything that involves the team.

CLIMATE IN ACTION 6.4

A great example of a coach who understood this is Bengt Johansson, one of the most successful handball coaches in the history of Sweden. He coached the national team to two World Championships (plus four more silver/bronze medals), four European championships, and three silver Olympic medals. What was exceptional about his coaching (besides his athletes' long-term success on the court), was his approach of valuing his athletes' input. He wrote a book about strategies the National Team could use, but felt it was worthless until he asked his athletes for feedback about the content. He grew to treat his athletes as "assistant coaches" and saw how they became more absorbed in the game, shared more of their ideas, and this resulted in Johansson growing as a coach and the team getting better (Annerstedt & Lingren, 2014).[2]

- **Giving all athletes opportunities to lead and share their talents with the team.** Coaches can help athletes feel important to the team when they are on the lookout for how to utilize the talents of each member. Think about how fun it is for athletes if they are asked to use their art skills to help paint a mural in the locker room, lead the discussion in a time-out, or develop and explain a drill that the team does in practice. Coaches can be creative in thinking about how to incorporate athletes' talents. Maybe athletes write an imagery script (describing the team's inspired play) that they could read aloud on the bus ride to a competition, or maybe on a practice or game day an athlete plays guitar (or another instrument) that helps athletes focus or relax. Maybe an athlete does research on nutritional intake for athletes and makes healthy snacks for the team, plans ahead for where the team can eat meals while at tournaments (selecting restaurants that have healthy choices), puts examples of menus together that would provide strong fuel for the team during the season, or shares information about well known athletes that take their nutrition seriously. Maybe athletes offer to work with younger/lower skilled athletes on the weekend, getting together to do drills and offer encouragement. One karate Sensei (coach) we know uses athletes of different ages to demonstrate. An experienced 9-year-old may be asked to demonstrate a skill that an 18-year-old who is new to the program is learning. The possibilities are endless for how coaches can help athletes utilize their talents and interests to benefit the team.
- **Watch and discuss a movie together that highlights important roles individuals have played in sport or in other areas of life.** One of our favorite movies to bring home this point is Jack Black's "School of Rock." This light-hearted comedy is about a young man with an incredible passion

for rock music who finds himself substitute teaching in a selective private school. He quickly veers from teaching the curriculum, and instead spends the entire school day helping the students create a rock band with all the important support groups (back-up singers, groupies, costumes, light and sound board, etc.). Black's character is all in with regard to valuing the contribution of each of his students. The band cannot be all it can be without the full effort of every supporting role. It is a funny movie, with a definite message about the important roles we all play in different areas of our lives, and how rewarding it is to be part of a group where everyone takes their roles seriously.

- **Give athletes opportunities to notice the important contributions of their teammates**. Coaches can be creative in thinking of activities they can do that allow athletes to identify ways in which their teammates are important to the team. Athletes can be encouraged to share their kudos with teammates verbally or via writing.

    o **Make a card for a teammate.** On a rainy day or a holiday (Martin Luther King, Jr. Day; Valentine's Day) athletes could draw the name of a teammate (out of a hat) and make a card for that person. Athletes can be encouraged to write and describe ways in which their teammates are important to the team. Coaches could bring nice paper, pens, markers, etc. and allow athletes to be creative in preparing their cards. At the end of the session, athletes could present their homemade cards to their teammates. Some teams may find it motivating to read aloud the cards they wrote for their teammates but some might prefer to keep it private. There are many versions of this activity. Every athlete could have a sheet of paper with their name at the bottom, and sitting in a circle, the sheets could be passed around, giving each athlete a chance to write an anonymous comment on the sheet. After a comment is added, the athlete who wrote it can fold the paper over and pass it to the next person in the circle. Another way to do this is to tape small posters on the wall and allow athletes to circulate and write comments on each of their teammates' posters. The aim in all these activities is to help athletes support one another.

    o **Share kudos to teammates publicly.** At the end of practice or competition, coaches could give athletes an opportunity to speak aloud a compliment to a teammate. Athletes would have a chance to give a shout out to their teammates and might say things like,

        - *"Lisa, way to rebound all night long. Wow, that was big for the team."*
        - *"Chung-Soo, you threaded a needle with those throws today. Excellent job."*
        - *"Mikayla, it was huge how you kept your composure after the official missed that call; great show of sportspersonship."*
        - *"Andy, thanks for talking to me when I came out of the game. You really helped me feel confident."*

- *"Brendan, thanks for noticing the pitcher has a hitch when he throws his curveball. I wouldn't have noticed that if you had not said something to me."*

  When athletes hear these kinds of statements it can help them feel valued by their teammates, more connected and engaged, and stimulate a desire to work hard.

o **Avoid MVP Awards.** Sometimes at end of the season ceremonies, athletes are selected to receive "MVP" awards, and the implication is that particular athletes are more important to the team than others. This approach to sport has been around a long time, and has come to be the norm and what everyone expects to happen at the end of a season. We would suggest that coaches who are creating a caring and task-involving climate need to align all that they do within this framework. Identifying an athlete as most valuable to the team is contradictory to the philosophy that every athlete plays an important role.

o **Recognize the contribution of the assistant coaches.** Head coaches can have very different relationships with their assistant coaches. Some assistant coaches have particular roles (e.g., keeping stats during games) and others seem to float around in the background. When head coaches make clear their view that assistant coaches are important to the team, it sends a strong message to athletes that they, too, should appreciate their coaches. When head coaches speak about the coaching staff in terms of "we" instead of "I," athletes are reminded that their head coaches see the assistants as their esteemed colleagues.

o **Recognize other members of the program.** In addition to helping athletes see how their teammates are important to the program, coaches can also expand this approach to include all parties that help the team. These might include bus drivers, administrators, tournament directors, parents, maintenance/janitorial staff, etc. One team makes sure every bus driver has a hat and t-shirt with the team's logo. Another team has the habit of doing a cheer on the bus when they return from a trip that thanks the driver. They describe how the driver does not show a lot of emotion when the team does it, but one athlete overheard the driver talking on the phone and describing what the team does and how much fun it is to drive for the team. Teaching athletes to have gratitude is an important skill in helping them recognize how to see the important role that people in their lives play for them.

*****

When coaches embrace this feature of the climate, that Every Athlete Plays an Important Role on the team, the door is open to be creative and to find many,

many strategies to reinforce these ideas for their team. It would be great to ask athletes, coaching friends, and others how this feature has come to life on teams they have been part of in the past.

Coaches can highlight these individuals' contributions to the team, and go further to have athletes personally thank them, write notes of gratitude, or find other ways to recognize their efforts. These kinds of activities help athletes develop the skill of being able to notice what others are doing well, get into a habit of sharing these observations with their teammates, and they bring fun and positive energy to the team. Above all, they remind athletes that every one of these individuals is important to the team.

Reflecting on Practice

Consider the ideas presented in this chapter and reflect upon how you might incorporate them into your own coaching practice. Here are a few ideas to get you started:

Coach Lead Behaviors

- What important roles do each of your athletes play on your team? What qualities and attributes do they bring to the team?
- How do you convey the importance of each athlete to the group? What kinds of things do you say and what behaviors do you engage in to send these messages that all athletes are important?
- What would your athletes say if asked if their coach noticed and valued their contributions to the team?
- Do your words and actions differ based on whether you are interacting with your best athletes versus those with lower skills?

Helping Athletes Appreciate One Another

- How do you go about helping your athletes develop an appreciation for one another? How do they reinforce the concept that all athletes are valuable to the team?
- What kinds of strategies on your part have worked well, and what are areas that you would like to improve?
- What ideas in this chapter might you implement to help athletes see how each member of the team is important?

Sources

1   Becker, A. & Wrisburg, C. (2008). Effective coaching in action: Observations of legendary collegiate basketball coach Pat Summitt. *The Sport Psychologist, 22,* 197–211.

2   Annerstedt, C. & Lingren, E. (2014). Caring as an important foundation in coaching for social sustainability: A case study of a successful Swedish coach in high performance sport. *Reflective Practice: International and Multidisciplinary Perspectives, 15,* 27–39.

7

FEATURES OF A CARING AND TASK-INVOLVING CLIMATE IN SPORT

Cooperation Among Teammates is Fostered and Valued

Highlights

* Coaches help athletes learn to work together as a team (striving together versus rivalry).
* Coaches emphasize helping one another and challenging each other to become better athletes.
* Coaches nurture and model cooperation on their team.
* Coaches cooperate with athletes by allowing joint decision making.
* Coaches structure player-centered practices and use the games approach to foster cooperation, autonomy, and decision-making.

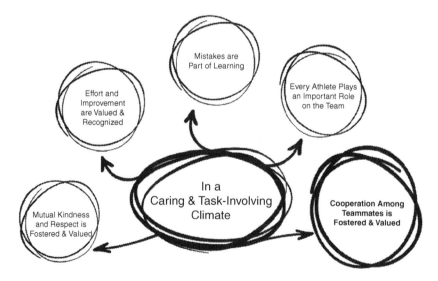

"Good teams become great ones when the members trust each other enough to surrender the 'me' for the 'we'" – *Phil Jackson, Basketball* [1]

In our quest to pursue sporting excellence and accomplish personal goals while being part of a sports team, it is not uncommon to instinctively develop a perspective that prioritizes the "me" (such as when a coach being interviewed at the end of the game says: *"I told the team to stay on the attack and it showed that my strategy was perfect and successful"* or when an athlete proudly yells: *"What a pass I gave you, Elia! Just brilliant! No wonder you got the ball in and scored!"*) over the "we" (*"I am really pleased with the effort we came out with. We started the game with a ton of energy and were persistent on the attack"* [coach] or *"Gals, we were focused, coordinated, talking to each other and got the ball through the net, what a team!"* [athlete]). When "me" eclipses "we," as mirrored in these examples, the focus turns to rivalry or animosity, reflected in the actions of the participants, as opposed to working together in unity to accomplish the team goal. As highlighted in Chapter 1, fostering and valuing cooperation among teammates is at the core of a caring and task-involving climate. As the leader of the team, coaches are the compass for their athletes' actions and, as such, have the potential to greatly impact the team by setting the tone and creating a team culture that tells the athletes that on this team we work together and support each other so everyone flourishes and succeeds. This chapter provides ideas that coaches can implement to help create this kind of environment and nurture and model cooperation on their teams.

How Coaches Communicate Cooperation

Coaches reflect on the values and beliefs that are important to them, which then guide their actions. One of those actions involves helping athletes work together toward a common goal. This requires coaches and athletes to value and foster cooperation on their team. Sometimes this can be difficult as sports are often defined by the outcome of the game. However, coaches want their athletes to focus on the process of learning and getting better at their sport and to convey a culture that "on this team" we support each other and we want athletes to see each practice or game as a place to work together, learn from and with each other, and develop skills as a team.

Consider how the following messages delivered to two athletes in the same situation will be received and, most importantly, how the coaches' words will impact each athlete, on the receiving end of the message (See Table 7.1).

How will Karli feel after talking to the coach in each case? Hearing Coach Dean talk about the tournament as just one more opportunity to play well and strengthen her skills will likely put her at ease and looking forward to competition. Working together with her teammate will be a fun and helpful way to prepare, get insight and be challenged and ready. Chances are that she will not approach the tournament as a stressful event when hearing the coach's confidence in her

TABLE 7.1 Modeling Rivalry vs. Cooperation

Rivalry focus	Cooperative focus
Coach Joe:	Coach Dean:
"Hey, with just a day to get to the tournament, I want everyone to practice extra hard, focus on polishing your skills, clean passes, no mistakes. Karli, pay attention to Hayley, she is doing those great twists and turns to defend the goal; she is on top of her game! Remember that I can only put the best of you on the field to maximize our chances. I will be watching each one of you and finalizing the startup team for tomorrow based on who performs the best today in practice."	*"Hey, I know the tournament is just around the corner. Remember that the only thing you need to do, Karli, is play good soccer, which you know how to do, right? Karli, why don't you pair up with Hayley, so you can help each other catch those minor mistakes together now instead of tomorrow at the game... push each other a bit and share feedback so you are both looking great when it gets your turn to defend the goal. Hayley, why don't you give Karli some tips to get those great twists and turns?"*

skills and her value to the team. On the other hand, Coach Joe, conveying the message that promotes competition, in which outperforming others and rivalry is salient, may make Karli not feel very connected to Hayley and even become hostile toward her (even though Hayley had no part in the discussion except by being portrayed as a rival in the message). Feeling the pressure from the coach and being compared to Hayley may make Karli worry about the outcome of the game, feel anxious, and not look forward to competing. In essence, it is important to consider the impact communication patterns play in fostering or undermining cooperation on sport teams.

Coaching Practices that Foster Cooperation

Of course, coaches are the ones who know best what may work with their team to foster cooperation; however, below are some ideas to create a team culture that focuses on helping one another accomplish goals together.

Model Cooperative Behavior

From a coach perspective, one of the most rewarding things to see in athletes is that they have not only mastered sport skills but also have developed life skills that will be extremely useful in their future careers. To enhance life skill development, one coaching goal could be to intentionally develop leadership and self-direction by giving athletes opportunities to make their own decisions without being told what to do. It is not always easy to release power but doing so models cooperation on the part of the coach. In other words, it sends the message that coaches trust athletes enough to have them take a more active role on the team. A small move coaches can take in this direction is to have a different athlete lead the warm-up each practice, check attendance to make sure everyone has arrived, or give athletes a say in what play or drill they would like to work on during practice. As the athletes learn to accept increasing responsibility coaches can let them take a turn being a "coach for the day" or being an "assistant coach." Not only does this foster their leadership skills and personal responsibility but it also enhances motivation. The team will also realize that coaching is not as easy as it seems and athletes may further value their coach's effort. Skills like organization and communication may be developed. Athletes may also surprise coaches by starting practice on a day when the coach runs into traffic or has an emergency and arrives a bit late to practice!

Seek Feedback From Athletes

Another way to foster cooperation is by seeking feedback from athletes. For example, whenever a timeout is called, a volleyball coach can meet with her assistants and then walk over to the team and ask one simple question, "*I called a timeout because I think we need to adapt to our opponent. What do you think we need to do to adapt?*" The coach then listens to her athletes, considers their insights in combination with the feedback provided by her assistants, steps into the huddle and provides her instructions and encouragement. The athletes in this example will feel valued and empowered by having their comments heard. They are also a lot more likely to be fully engaged in the game. They understand that the coach has the last word but having a voice may bring everyone together and determined to succeed. Coach Manoli in Hudson, Ohio, has his own variation on this. As the game is progressing he walks up and back along the bench, asking players who are not in the game their opinions on what needs to occur on the court. During timeouts the coach will refer to those interactions by saying "*Jason noticed we're not boxing out on the weak side. C'mon, now, let's focus on that. Jason, keep an eye on that for me.*" This sends a powerful message to the athletes. Everyone's opinion and contribution is valued. The reason the team is doing well is because everyone is cooperating and everyone is contributing.

Ideas Coaches Can Use that Reflect a Cooperative Approach and Promote Working Together Regardless of Athlete's Talent or Seniority in the Team

Encourage Athletes to Support Each Other During Competitions

Part of working together is learning to support one another during competitions. Coaches can let athletes know that an important role everyone plays on the team is being a team player. Coaches can emphasize to the athletes how important it is to their teammates on the field to hear them cheering from the sidelines. Here are a few examples for coaches to consider:

- Coaches can encourage athletes to support their teammates' performance from the bench (as shown in the previous examples) or provide feedback and tell them they value their effort on the field when they come out during substitutions. For example, "*High five, Lori! You were on a roll today stealing and dribbling those balls!*" Players on the sideline can also be supportive by yelling, "*Great communication!*" or advice that focuses their attention on something they may miss, such as, "*Watch your back*" or perhaps help them move on from their mistakes quickly with a "*Good try, no worries, try again!*" or "*No big deal; keep it up!*"

- Coaches can encourage athletes to use a word or mental symbol to represent letting go of a mistake and putting it out of mind, such as mimicking throwing an invisible paper ball over their left shoulder meaning "*it is gone*" or shout "*park it!*" meaning it is in the past and out of their mind. One soccer team created some 'team' symbols themselves that made sense to them and which they could use to communicate in the field and help a teammate regain focus after a mistake. Right after a bad pass that ended on the feet of an opponent Jess would call to Clara and yell 'park it' to call her attention to refocus.

- Coaches can ask athletes how they can support their teammates. They may come up with things like: "*I can let them know they have a player behind them that they don't see*" or just shout "*Great pass!*" or "*Good idea!*" so that they keep their confidence up and feel everyone is working together and has each other's back.

Coaches can remind athletes that while there are some teams that stay quiet on the bench just watching, it is easy to create a team culture both when they are playing and on the sidelines. Once the players see how good it feels to hear the cheering from afar and know the team is with them, silence from the bench will quickly become a thing of the past.

Implement Peer Mentoring

Coaches can pair more senior athletes with new athletes to give them an opportunity to connect and work together while transmitting this "team" philosophy to new players. Mentoring can be very informal or more organized, depending on time and what works in the program. It can range from having older athletes being a 'buddy' by showing her the ropes, getting to know people, and filling her in on how the team works, or having a more structured mentoring program. An example of a more structured program is to have sophomores connect with and mentor the new first year class. The sophomores can share their own experiences of when they arrived to the program (which would still be fresh in their minds) and share some strategies that worked well for them, such as talking to the coach when they have issues, asking the team when they are confused or need to know where to go, etc. A first year class may feel impatient with not being able to play games yet, get discouraged and doubt their ability. Sophomores can assure them that this is typical in the first year and that coaches are making sure they transition well and that they will work with them so they are ready which will lead to success for them on the field. Similarly, coaches could pair seniors with juniors, so athletes that are leaving the program can share insight with the rising leaders that will help them be stronger leaders. Working together through these transitions makes athletes feel that this team supports each other and that they work together to keep the team strong.

CLIMATE IN ACTION 7.1

A way to have athletes work together is used by Coach Pat, a local soccer coach. He had Noah, a more mature player with a lot of experience, pair up with Paul, who just moved in and joined the club but had not played a game yet. They sat together on the sidelines and Noah would go over aspects Paul would need to pay attention to once he gets in, what players have more experience and what to watch out for, and emphasize how everyone in this league is a team player and he'll get into the swing of things in no time. This helped Paul be ready and confident in his first game with a new team.

Encourage Your Team to Push and Challenge Each Other in Practices

Coaches can create some games or strategies to encourage athletes to challenge themselves during practices so they become better players. A coach can group teammates that play the same position and have them brainstorm about the challenges or pressures of being a defender or a midfielder, for example, then ask them to work together to come up with ideas to make 'the job' easier and be more effective. Sharing ideas and working together will help create a bond with those who share the same positions, instead of having athletes see each other as someone competing for the same position on game night. Coaches can also mention how they have been finishing games on double overtime and share ideas on how they can deal with that. Helen may say, "*Well, I think if we motivate each other to get fit during the week those long games will get easier.*" or "*If we train those plays together in practice we will be more confident to shoot when we have seconds left.*" If athletes push and support each other to get better, they will all improve and be ready to step up to the plate if someone gets injured or the need arrives. Another simple yet effective strategy to help athletes' support each other's goals, challenge teammates, and foster camaraderie and teammate accountability is the *Support Squad*, developed by Jeff Janssen (Janssen, 1991, p.146).[2] This team building activity involves pairing athletes at the start of the week, have them each write their goals for that week and then brainstorm potential obstacles they could think of that may prevent them from achieving their goal; then, together, come up with ideas of ways to overcome those obstacles and things that each one can do to assist their teammate. Beyond its simplicity, this exercise is a great idea to support and keep teammates focused on the goals during practice and competition.

Nurture Cooperation Regardless of the Athletes' Assigned Position

One way to make sure that the team becomes a tight knit group is to make sure that everyone understands that together the team is stronger and that every athlete's contribution is important (Chapter 6 focused on this feature). While it is explicit and agreed that every position in each sport is important, some positions are more visible (in soccer, forwards score the goal but often a midfielder has made the pass to the forward). Therefore, it is important that athletes realize that the entire team needs to work together to achieve the team goals, regardless of position. A good drill to do in practice to help everyone understand each other's value is to switch positions in practice. For example, by putting Sam, who is a forward, in place of Ignasi, who is a defender, Sam will experience the pressure and challenge of keeping his attention broad to scan the field and cover one or more players so that Ignasi can run to the goal and shoot; or Sam can also see that sometimes there is a need for forwards to perhaps move up at times in defense. Similarly, having all positions switch with the goalie at times, is also useful, as game situations may need a field player to cover for a goalie due to injury. In fact, we know of a college soccer team where the primary goalie suffered a season long injury a few weeks before the semifinal game and was replaced by the second goalie. As luck had it, she got injured 15 minutes before the end of the game. Without hesitation, one of the captains (who played the position of a forward) put the gloves on and walked to secure the goal. She told her teammates to keep focused and she was able to avoid any goals by the opposing team. That is a great example of leadership and working together to help the team. Switching positions can be a valuable exercise for athletes to become more empathic and understanding of others' challenges and working better together.

Structuring Player-Centered Practices to Foster Cooperation, Empowerment, and Decision-Making

So far this chapter has highlighted the essence of fostering cooperation in sport teams as a tenet of a caring and task-involving climate, and also underlined practical examples to show how coaches can model, nurture, and foster cooperation. One further reflection is to consider how coaches can use 'the game' itself to infuse an atmosphere of cooperation in which athletes learn not only from the coach, but also from themselves and from one another.

One teaching method that is consistent with the feature of fostering cooperation and working together is the *games approach to coaching* [3,4] (similarly known as *teaching games for understanding*). One reason why this approach is a good fit is because it has a predominantly *player-centered* approach to coaching (which is compatible with a caring climate). From this view, the coaches' role is more aligned with that of a *facilitator*; coaches adjust activities for success or challenge, acknowledge good play, and often participate with players instead of being a direct teacher (who would adjust activities or verbally shape ideas to bring out training goals and rarely participates with the players). The athlete role, in turn, is more of an *active participant* who, instead of being told what to do and learn, goes through a *guided self-discovery* to learn what to do and how to do it *within the context of the game*. Helping athletes understand "why" to decide one option or another, such as shoot or pass, is the most important aspect of teaching for understanding. In reality, "coaches who routinely tell athletes *what to do* can be quite successful in the short term, while coaches who *help athletes process situations* help develop independent thinkers who are better-able to solve both predictable and novel problems."[5] This method of coaching, which coaches may already be using with their teams, may need some practice because the coach questions need to be framed in ways that can lead players to process the learning on their own. For example, here are two different questions a coach can ask: "*Where did the ball ended up Marc?*," Marc: "*Over the bar.*" Or the coach could ask instead "*Do you know why the ball went over the bar?*" Marc: "*I kicked the bottom of the ball and got under it too much.*" While both questions are good, the second made Marc think deeper and arrive at the understanding on his own. In essence, the role of the coach when coaching through a games approach method is to "guide" the athlete to understand what he cannot process on his own and lets athletes realize on their own what to do by experiencing and being part of the game. Since young athletes love playing the real game, learning and practicing the skill in a gamelike situation is highly motivating, empowering and effective. In the end, designing player-centered practices not only impacts each player individually but also encourages teammates to work together in simulated game situations where they rely more on one another.

How Can Coaches Incorporate this Approach into their Coaching?

The main point of the games approach is to structure a practice in a way that mimics the game situation as much as possible. Coaches can *modify the game* to maximize success and challenge to all players while creating realistic, gamelike, and challenging training activities on their teams. Coaches can achieve this by modifying the play in three ways: *shaping the play*, meaning using the game itself to teach athletes game situations (for example, placing two offensive players against one defensive player like the fast-break drill in basketball), *focusing the play*, which simply means teaching your players to be focused on a particular aspect you want them to learn (such as learning to be aware of their teammates' position to see who to pass to or how to create open space) and third, *enhancing the play*, which refers to presenting challenges or using handicapping techniques to make close contests.

Examples of *shaping* the play include things like redesigning the game so that athletes have the opportunity to practice what is relevant, develop awareness of how to make a goal or a basket, create small-sided games to help less experienced players learn at ease and develop more confidence, or instead, create a larger-sided game to help experienced players create more scoring chances.

Focusing the play aims at just that! Have athletes focus on critical elements of the game, explain the purpose of a play or practice, label key elements to be learned, remind players of these actions, stop play to ask athletes questions about recognizing things they (or their teammates) could do differently, correct mistakes on their own and reinforce the correct action (freeze replay).

Examples of *enhancing* the play may be a coach creating rules to stress particular skills, such as passing, by requiring three passes before a player can shoot or setting limitations such as that only certain players can score. In general, coaches can modify play by altering the number of players, the size and shape of the field, the duration of the play, the scoring method or adding special rules.

Below are some ideas coaches can try to modify the game and encourage athletes to learn together. The examples here are framed from soccer but you can adapt them to baseball, hockey or similar sports.

- **Re-shuffle teams after every round.** By doing this your athletes will get the chance to play with all their teammates, getting to know each other and learn different styles and techniques from all.
- **Manipulate the number of players.** Having less players on your team will increase repetition, learning and action while larger numbers on your team means fewer opportunities for each player to be active providing for more rest periods and less fitness.
- **If the score becomes lopsided.** Coaches can solve a lopsided score by adding players to the losing team, changing the higher skilled player with the goalkeeper, or removing a player from the winning team. Coaches can modify the game to always aim at making it competitive and challenging.
- **Use the 'freeze' effectively for guided self-discovery.** This technique has significant value as a coaching tool when the coach goes beyond stopping the play to merely provide the correct instruction to instead leading the athletes in a self-reflection on their actions, develop an understanding of the game and being able to arrive at a better option of play. How this looks in practice is that a coach observing a play will give a sign to the athletes to stop where they are (known as *freeze*) and asks them to *rewind* to the moment where an action happened that the coach wants athletes to re-think and come up with a better option. Players reposition themselves to that moment and are asked to identify the missed cue that resulted in the poor decision: "*Julia, what did you see before the ball arrived?*," "*What is this situation telling you?*"; include others in the

conversation: "*What could anyone else have done to help Julia?*" The coach then restarts the game with Julia choosing an alternative solution: "*C'mon Julia, here's the ball, try something else.*" or "*Here is the ball, let's keep it in our team.*" The overall aim of this learning exercise is for the athletes to understand the game and be able to apply decision making that supports and helps each other.

Essentially, the focus of this approach is to help athletes understand the game and then help each other learn it from themselves and from each other. Coaches that implement the games approach in their practices quickly note that it is highly motivating for their athletes, encourages all athletes to think and come up with ideas to better accomplish the team's objectives, fosters autonomy, empowerment and builds team chemistry.

From Coach Modeling and Fostering Cooperation to Athlete Learning and Integrating Cooperation

One of the most fulfilling moments for coaches is seeing how modeling particular positive behaviors and structuring the coaching environment to promote positive actions results in their athletes' assimilating and embracing such behavior. An example of this idea is reflected in Madison, a team captain, who, during a discussion about what everyone thought should be their team goals for the season shared that the team was awesome and she wanted to win a championship, not just to win, but to do so with that group because they were in it together. Madison did not want to win just to win, but because for her it was the culmination of their development together into a great team (skill and people).

Another illustration epitomizing the impact coaches' have on their athletes was the story of Central Washington softball team working together with their opposing team of Western Oregon to help one of their players. For readers not familiar with this story, this is what took place that day. Sara Tucholsky, a senior player with Western Oregon hit the first home run of her college career, in a crucial game for advancing to the playoffs. Sadly, on her home run trot Sara missed first base and when she turned back to touch the base her knee bent and she went down crawling to first base (later learning she had torn her ACL). Seeing Sara on the ground and learning from the umpire that should she be assisted by any person of her team she would be penalized, Mallory Holtman, a player for Central Washington asked if she could help by carrying her around as Sara touched the bags. Asked afterwards why she did it, Mallory simply stated that she had been taught by her coach that "winning is not everything."[6] Undoubtedly, when coaches teach athletes to cooperate and help one another, they are teaching them long-lasting life skills.

A similar yet less known story to show how young athletes integrate the value of working together and helping each other while competing is the one of Ashley

Barter, an Australian high school cross country runner who in the midst of her race saw one of her opponents struggling to run due to a high ankle sprain. Ashley ran alongside her opponent and when she saw the injured runner slow down she did the same. She later explained that she did that because she wanted her runmate to finish, so she went back and ran by her side until they both crossed the finish line together.[7]

Not only are these examples of developing a positive perspective to competition and excellence gratifying for coaches who intentionally implement and nurture a positive sport climate but, from a practical standpoint, developing this climate is also helpful to coaches. Once athletes integrate certain values (such as fostering cooperation and working together), they also contribute to the team culture that coaches are instilling. In essence, coaches then have these team ambassadors who are helping nurture the team, minimizing conflict, and helping all athletes have a more positive sport experience, so it seems to be a win–win situation!

*****

This chapter highlights the relevance of having a coaching philosophy and a team culture that emphasizes learning to cooperate among teammates and helping one another develop their skills as a team. We stress that the coach's role in nurturing and modeling cooperation in their teams is core to foster these values within their teams and develop character in their athletes. We argue that structuring player-centered practices that foster cooperation, autonomy, and decision making among athletes will result in effective learning and more highly motivated athletes.

Reflecting on Practice

Reflecting and developing self-awareness of your day to day coaching practices and considering how your practice aligns with your views and philosophy as a coach may be a useful self-assessment of how you coach. Steered by the ideas introduced in this chapter, below are some questions that may be used to reflect on how you emphasize and incorporate some of the ideas described into your coaching.

Self-reflection

- How do I keep a perspective in my practice that prioritizes the "we" over the "me" with my athletes and teams? What are some drills I use in practice that highlight the idea of working together as a team?
- In what ways do I infuse a team atmosphere that highlights unity and working together to accomplish the team goals?
- How do I ensure that everybody feels part of this team, knows each other and that nobody feels left out?
- What are some ways in which I promote cooperation both in practices and games?
- Do my actions and communication convey that I value cooperation and helping each other change in to on this team? What are some things I say to my athletes that transmit that idea?
- How do I convey to my athletes the value of focusing on the process of learning instead of portraying success defined by the outcome of the game? What are actions I see in my athletes that tell me that my athletes understand that value?
- How do I communicate to the team that rivalry and animosity among my athletes is discouraged? What are some things I tell my athletes to support that?
- What are ways in which I model cooperation in my coaching and to my athletes?
- Do I intentionally develop autonomy and decision-making with my athletes?
- How do I structure practices in a way that allows athletes to practice decision-making and autonomy?

Your reflection and answers to these questions may help you assess in what ways you are fostering a caring and task-involving climate in which cooperation among teammates is nurtured and valued.

Assessing Quality of Practice Session

Guided by the ideas presented in this chapter to nurture aspects such as cooperation, engagement or decision-making, you may consider reflecting on how things went during your practice session or competition using the questions below as a self-assessment of your coaching.

- How relevant were the activities I design in my practices for my goals for the team?
- Were my athletes given opportunity to be in control?
- In what ways did I engage players in guided discovery?
- Were all my players overcoached? Was I overly directive?
- What did I see from observing the athletes that showed their engagement in the activities?
- What were my goals for my players? How was my coaching helping them to become better?
- How was my feedback relevant and effective for the athlete? Did I provide accurate and timely feedback to all my athletes?
- What aspects of my practice helped every athlete to see progress?
- What aspects of my practice contribute to every athlete experiencing success?
- What kind of opportunities did I provide the athletes to work together?
- Were all my players active and engaged in practice?

Your answers to these questions will inform you about what things you do in your practices that create a quality and player-centered practice that develops physically active athletes, and self-directed and decision-making learners.

Athletes' Reflection on Being a Teammate

Reflecting and developing self-awareness of what kind of teammate your players are to others in terms of cooperation, support, and being able to work in unison with their teammates (all features described in this chapter) may be an effective exercise for your athletes. Below are some activities that coaches can use with their athletes to make them reflect on how they see themselves and others in relation to working together as a team. Coaches can have their athletes write their thoughts down (without names); then the coach collects and shares the answers provided by each team member and facilitates a group discussion in which the athletes contrast and debate the responses they hear from their teammates.

- Think about the best teammates that you have had across all your sport experiences. What qualities and behaviors made them strong and valued teammates in your view? How did they make their teammates better? What kinds of things did they do to support their teammates?
- Think about the worst teammates that you have had across all your sport experiences. What qualities and behaviors do you feel made them ineffective or unreliable teammates? What kinds of things did they do to show a lack of support of their teammates? How did they hurt the team?

- What are things you could do that you are not currently doing to consistently be a better teammate? How hard would it be for you to make these changes? What impact could it have for the team if every member strived to be a better teammate?
- Now think about how your teammates might describe you. Think about how they would describe your behavior in games, practices and outside of organized sport (maybe during school). Think about what they would say about your behavior, how you treat others, what you say, and your overall attitude.

Athletes' Journal Activity

Coaches may consider having athletes use a journal at the beginning or end of practice, before or after games, or at other times, based on what works best for the team. This should not be a lengthy activity, perhaps 10 to 15 min, depending on the athlete and how practice went that day and salient themes that came up for reflection. Athletes can write about what they could do to support their teammates on that day or about what actions they saw from their teammates that supported others. Or they may reflect and consider which teammates may need extra support. They could also brainstorm behaviors they want to engage in that will help the team on that day, and afterwards journal about how things went. This activity may be new for athletes, but once they understand how to do the activity it should focus everyone's attention on the power of having supportive teammates. Coaches could have a small composition notebook for each athlete that they keep in a box. This tool is actually widely used in the sport of rifle shooting with a focus on the athlete's reflection on what went well and what needed improvement and is one of the best ways to improve target accuracy.

Sources

[1]   Jackson, P. & Delehanty, H. (1995). *Sacred hoops: Spiritual lessons of a hardwood warrior* (1st ed.). New York, NY: Hyperion.

[2]   Janssen, J. (1999). *Championship team building: What every coach needs to know to build a motivated, committed, and cohesive team*. Tucson, AZ: Winning the Mental Game.

[3]   Launder, A. 2001. *Play practice: The games approach to teaching and coaching sport*. Champaign, IL: Human Kinetics.

[4]   Martens, R. (2010). The Games Approach. In *Successful Coaching* (4th ed., pp.149–160). Champaign, IL: Human Kinetics.

[5]   Turner, T. (April, 2018). *A question of style: Building a stronger club culture in Northern Ohio. A Curriculum*. Ohio North Youth Soccer Association. www.ohionorthsoccer.org

[6]   Vecsey, G. (2008, April 30). A sporting gesture touches 'em all. *The New York Times*, Retrieved from [A Sporting Gesture Touches 'Em All by George Vecsey, April 30, 2008;www.nytimes.com/2008/04/30/sports/baseball/30vecsey.html]

[7]   *True Sport*, Retrieved from [6 Great Examples of Sportsmanship https://learn.truesport.org/6-great-examples-of-sportsmanship/]

PART III

Special Considerations in Creating a Caring and Task-Involving Climate in Sport

8

PLANNING FOR AND DEVELOPING A CARING AND TASK-INVOLVING CLIMATE THROUGHOUT THE SEASON

Highlights

- Before the season starts, coaches can be intentional about developing a plan to reinforce a caring and task-involving climate across the season.
- Many coaches describe starting strong at the beginning of the season, but catch themselves fading out with emphasizing the features of a caring and task-involving climate as the season goes along.
- Coaches can implement many strategies mid- and post-season that would keep athletes having strong perceptions of a caring and task-involving climate.

In Section 2 of the book we discussed each of the features of a caring and task-involving climate, giving coaches many ideas for bringing the climate to life. In this chapter we provide strategies for coaches who are trying to get a strong jump out of the gates to begin creating a caring and task-involving climate from the first team meeting. We have many ideas both for bringing out the features of a caring and task-involving climate early in the season so that athletes, parents, bus drivers, and all involved learn about the team's core philosophy and approach, and for carrying that climate throughout the season. Some coaches tell us that they do a good job in the beginning but would like to be more intentional about continuing those strategies every single day of the season.

Activities to Start the Season Creating a Caring and Task-Involving Climate

- **Tryouts.** We will start with what occurs first for some teams and that is tryouts. One thing we hear often from young athletes that makes us sad is when they tell us they aren't trying out for a sport team when they would really like to play the sport. *"I don't know if I'm good enough to make the team"*; *"Some of the people trying out for the team are pretty mean"*; and *"The coach seems intimidating"* are some of the reasons young people give us for avoiding tryouts all-together. It should be the case that, after tryouts, regardless of outcomes, athletes would be saying, *"Tryouts were really fun"*; *"The coaches are great"*; *"I'm glad I tried out"*; and *"It wasn't as bad as I thought it might be."*

The truth is that tryouts can be a stressful, downer experience for young athletes who are not selected on teams. We believe that sometimes youth can get so worked up about tryouts that it actually affects their performance, making them less likely to make the team. That is, sometimes the best young athletes might not even make the team because they are so worried about making mistakes and performing poorly. Here are some things to think about for coaches who are in a position to run tryouts for their teams. First, it should be explained to youth at the first meeting what the goals of tryouts are and how tryouts will be run. Sometimes coaches have too many youth trying out for teams and too few spots and uniforms. By keeping too many youth it might be a disservice to all the youth if overall kids would not get much playing time. On the other hand, schools that have no-cut policies are showing many positive outcomes in terms of better attendance at school, greater student engagement, and higher physical activity levels, so coaches should do all they can to include as many youth as possible, and to look for alternative programs that might be in place or created to include greater numbers of athletes.

o   Here are several "speeches" that we feel would be important to share with all athletes.

   • **Setting up try-outs**. The coach states, *"Hello athletes, thank you for trying out for our team. We (the coaching staff) love this great game of ___ _____, and we appreciate that you must also. Look to your left and right and all around, and smile thinking about how fun it is to be around people who all love the same sport. We have _____ slots on the team, and unfortunately, we won't be able to keep every athlete here today on our squad this season. We sure wish we could, but here's what we are going to do. We have some drills set up we want you all to go through the next few days. We want to stress that we have never had athletes who didn't make mistakes. In fact, we coaches make lots of mistakes, so we don't want you to worry if you make a bad throw, swing at a bad pitch, etc. We want everyone to give us their best effort, have some fun, and get to know each other. One of the things we are looking at is what kind of teammates you would be. We like athletes that really support each other, and do all they can to help each other feel welcome and be the best that they can be. We are unimpressed when athletes try to show up their teammates or act all superior- there's no place for that on this team. We look forward to getting to know all of you over the next few days.*

Let's all relax, have some fun, and see what happens. For those who don't make the team in the end, we will be speaking with each of you individually and helping you have a game plan for how you can get better, and make the team in the future. There might be roles as managers, etc., that some of you might be interested in."

Our experience is that few coaches highlight the features of a caring and task-involving climate in their instructions about tryouts, and how amazing it is for young athletes to get this information early. It can help relieve pressure to perform better than others and lessen fear of failure, and also help young athletes have a positive tryout experience.

- **Wrapping up tryouts.** The coach states, *"We've had a super week of tryouts and we appreciate all of you coming out. It's been great to get to know you. We have loved seeing your high effort and commitment. We really enjoy coaching because of athletes like you who try hard to be the best they can be. We're going to start individual meetings with each of you where we can fill you in on our decisions and talk about next steps. For those of you who didn't make the team, we have ideas for how you can work on your skills and get better, and we will share these with you. Please know that we wish we could keep every athlete who has tried out. We hope that all of you will make connections at school, and continue to support one another, and stop by and keep in touch with us (the coaches). Any questions?"*

This approach to tryouts can soften the blow for some young athletes who do not make the team, and give them direction and hope for the future.

We have watched many youth sport tryouts where we wish the coaches could have had background information on the athletes. One athlete had parents who were very busy professionally and had little time to spend with their daughter. Another athlete had a sibling that was battling cancer, which took the majority of the parents' attention. Another lived with a single parent who was struggling with substance abuse. Another had parents who had just announced their plans to divorce. In each of these cases, it would have been great if the coach could have offered more words of encouragement, especially for those athletes who were not selected for the team. It is easy for young athletes to take things personally and also generalize, meaning that if they failed in one area they will likely fail in other areas. A little bit of exposure to a caring and task-involving climate and encouragement can go a long way to help young people feel connected and empowered. Even brief exposure to a supportive environment might make young people more willing to try or pursue other sports or physical activities in the future. Following such exposure, some youth might find it fun to be part of the team in other ways by serving as a manager, assistant to the coaches, an announcer in games, or keeping the statistics, running the scoreboard, or any number of helpful roles that might support the team. Young people need activities that keep them engaged and challenged, and in a caring and task-involving climate there are many roles to be filled.

CLIMATE IN ACTION 8.1

When I was coaching I can remember large numbers of kids trying out, and it was a tough decision where to draw the line on how many I could keep. I had a parent call me one afternoon during tryouts and she just wanted to get a feel for whether her son might make the JV tennis team. She knew he was going to be devastated if he did not make the team, and she wanted to know what was coming down the pike. She obviously was losing sleep because her son wanted to make the team so bad, and she knew that his skill level was likely inadequate to be able to make the team at a large high school. That conversation with that mother lead me to change my view about how I conducted tryouts with my tennis program. I started using an approach where I allowed every student to make the junior varsity team. It was crazy how many kids we started out the year with on this squad! Here was the catch though; if they were tardy three times during the semester they were removed from the team. It sounds harsh but the kids who didn't care that much ended up missing and drifting off, but the kids who really wanted to be there didn't miss (unless they were sick or had really good reasons). The student (whose mom called me) never missed and gave 100 percent. He definitely wasn't one of my more skilled athletes, but he sure improved due to his hard work. He definitely would have been one of the athletes who was cut from the team if I had conducted tryouts as usual. He gained so much from being on the team across his high school years. This "experiment" influenced my coaching philosophy. What was interesting is that it made coaching even more enjoyable because the kids who weren't as motivated weeded themselves out, and the athletes that were highly motivated were able to stick with the sport. I hope many coaches are thinking about these things when they structure tryouts. On the one hand, we coaches have to ask ourselves, why would we keep more athletes than we have uniforms for, or that will get to play in games? On the other hand, kids might benefit from being on a team with a strong, caring, and task-involving climate. When students do not have anything to do after school, it seems they can find trouble or engage in unproductive activities. Still, it was pretty exhausting to keep 40+ youngsters on a junior varsity tennis team with eight courts and one coach, but it was also crazy rewarding! If coaches were able to figure out a way to keep even two–three more athletes on their teams, what a difference this could make across schools, leagues, states, and the country.

Shared by Mary Fry

- **Introductions**. Another suggestion for coaches is to be creative in looking for ways to help all athletes get to know each other on the team. Sometimes coaches are so focused on sport specific activities, that it is easy to forget about the importance of helping athletes make connections with each other early in the season. Activities that help with introductions do not have to be time-consuming, they just need to be intentional. For example, coaches could:

  o **Emphasize the importance of getting to know your teammates**. Coaches can tell their athletes that it takes many teams half the season to get to know each other, and ask this, "*How can we be the team we want to be if it takes us half the season to get to know each other?*" Coaches can encourage athletes to be intentional about getting to know every athlete on the team.

  o **Take buddy breaks**. Take several water breaks or Buddy Breaks during practice and pair athletes up so that during the quick breaks (2 minutes), they connect with a teammate and talk about how their day was, how practice is going, their plans for the weekend, or anything that helps them get to know each other a little bit more. They can stick with a buddy for the day or switch it up so that they interact with different teammates each practice.

  o **Complete fact sheets**. Coaches can have athletes fill out sheets that have 25 facts about them and then at different moments (e.g., on the bus; at the end of practice), the coach can asked the team, "*Who on this team has been to Brazil?*" or "*Who on this team has met Michelle Obama?*" or "*Who on this team collects comic books?*" or "*Who on this team helps their grandparents with their apple orchard each year?*" and the team can guess who that athlete may be.

  o **Feature the pets**. Athletes can have a "Bring a picture of your pet(s) day" where they show off their pets and describe them to the team. Pets are important members of families and this activity helps athletes get to know something important about their teammates. If athletes do not have pets, they could bring a picture of a pet they hope to have one day. These pet pictures could even be featured on a bulletin board in the locker room.

  o **Bring in the jokes and quotes of the day**. Coaches could have a joke or quote of the day, and athletes could take turns sharing. It is good for athletes to have opportunities to talk in front of the team, and fun to hear from everyone and to see their senses of humor and the kind of quotes they find meaningful and why. Jokes like, "Why do frogs like to play baseball? ... Because they like to catch flies" keep things light and add a little humor to the day.

  o **Get to know athletes' families**. Coaches can encourage athletes to introduce their families to their teammates, and encourage teammates to make the effort to get to know their teammates' families. It could be that after a practice, athletes are paired up and they introduce each other to the parent who is there to pick them up. Athletes could be encouraged to say something like, "*Mom, I want to introduce you to Connor; he's a really good athlete and a friend on my team.*" This might lead to a 2-minute interaction where the parents have a connection now with one of their child's teammates.

o   **Learn names.** Coaches can set up drills where they call their teammates by name when they pass to them, receive a catch from them, etc.: "Lauren, it's coming"; "Thanks, Kylie." The drill does not have to last a long time, but even doing this for 5–10 minutes can help athletes learn their teammates' names.

o   **Experiment with social media.** Coaches might set up a group-me text that includes all the athletes on the team, and send positive messages out to the team every few days. Coaches might highlight the classy behavior of an athlete, the great performance of a team that worked together, or something in the news where a young person made a difference.

o   **Seek athletes' ideas for getting to know one another.** Another strategy coaches can use is to tell athletes that an important goal they have for the team is for all athletes to get to know every one of their teammates. The coach can describe how this is key to the team's success, and the coach can ask for suggestions for how the athletes think this can best happen. Athletes can have clever ideas and it sends a strong message that the coach is open to the athletes' suggestions for the team and values their contributions.

These are all quick and easy activities that coaches could use to help athletes get to know each other more quickly, have fun interacting with teammates, and get over the awkwardness of not knowing each other. We wish more coaches used these kinds of activities from the first day on. We observe many teams where athletes do not know everyone on the team until midseason, because no effort is made to facilitate the process.

• **Creating a team pact.** Another activity we recommend that coaches do is to help the team create a pact. This can be done as a group activity or it can be initiated by making it a station at practice. At this station, a coach or parent could help facilitate a discussion between athletes about the kind of team they would like to be and the kinds of teammates they would like to be for each other. Another way to phrase it sometimes is to have athletes think about what they would like to be able to say about their team at the end of the season, particularly in terms of the factors they have more control over. When given the opportunity, our experience is that athletes are quick to share things like they want to support their teammates and coaches during the ups and downs of the season, they want to give high effort, etc.

Table 8.1 is a pact a young baseball team, the DC Storm, made when they were about 10 years old. They all contributed ideas that were put into a brief pact that captured all their main goals. Many athletes had the same ideas of what they would like to see in their teammates, and after the discussions, all the ideas were put together in a final draft of the pact. The whole team discussed the final draft of the pact, and then tweaked, finalized and approved it all together. At a team meeting, each player took a pledge to do his best to honor the pact across the season, and it happened that these athletes played together for several seasons and continued to honor the pact they made in their first year together.

It may be surprising that 10-year-old athletes came up with this pact, but they did. It is easy to underestimate what young athletes are capable of, but creating a pact like this can play a huge role in helping youth sport be so much bigger than just providing a chance to play a sport for a short period. This team printed out the pact and laminated copies that athletes took home with them. The team was reminded of the pact throughout the season and encouraged to weigh in on how they were doing honoring the pact.

We have helped numerous teams at different levels of sport (youth, college) form pacts, and they have chosen different ways to initiate the pact. Sometimes teams have a ceremony where each athlete takes a pledge to do his/her best to honor the pact each day. Hearing one's teammates commit to being all in with regard to honoring the pact can be inspiring. Some teams have longer pacts and some have shorter ones. Teams have put a shortened version of their pact on a t-shirt, made candles (with words wrapped around the outside of the candle) to represent their pact, made a sign for their locker room that had the pact written on it and each member's handprint (made by dipping

TABLE 8.1 DC Storm Pact

DC Storm Pact
• We are positive and supportive of our teammates all the time.
• We are happy when our teammates do well.
• We stand by them when they make a mistake.
• When we make a mistake, we stay positive for the team.
• When the batting or field line-up isn't the way we prefer it, we stay positive.
• We get to know everyone on the team, their families, and the coaches.
• We give our best effort all the time (practice, games, etc.) in everything we do.
• We respect our opponents, and we act first class with them all the time.
• We support our coaches all the time, and we trust them to do their best for the team.

their hands in paint of the colors of their team). With this last one, the team touched the handprints when they entered and exited the locker room as a reminder of their commitment to upholding the pact.

Pacts are very difficult to honor across an entire season as athletes will face many challenges. An important aspect of the pact to emphasize for the team is that a pact is not in place so that athletes can point fingers at each other and note how their teammates are not doing an adequate job honoring the pact. Instead, the pact works best when everyone (coaches and athletes) understands that the pact is in place so that each individual can point fingers back at themselves and consider if they are honoring the pact to the best of their ability and how they could do so better. It is easy to assume that all young athletes understand the importance of the concepts covered in the pact, and that a pact is unnecessary, but the reality is that teams that talk about these concepts and put them on the table at the beginning of the season are more likely to have athletes that show respect for all involved in the sport.

Activities to Create a Caring and Task-Involving Climate Throughout the Season

In addition to running an effective round of tryouts, promoting fun introductions for the team, and creating a pact, the most important thing coaches can do is to continue building the caring and task-involving climate throughout the season, every single day. So here are some more ideas for what that might look like for coaches across the days and weeks of the season.

• **Keep making practice and competitions fun.** As the season progresses, it is not unusual for some teams to lose steam, especially if they are not having the success in terms of wins they had hoped for. Just like athletes, coaches can feel frustrated and beat up, so it is really critical for coaches to step back often and make sure they are doing all they can to help the team maintain their intensity, while having fun each day. In Climate in Action 8.2, Lindsey Fry describes a favorite volleyball coach (Wendel Carmaga) she had, and how his ability to have fun with the team was contagious.

CLIMATE IN ACTION 8.2

When I was in middle school, I had a volleyball coach named Wendel Camargo who was amazing. He made the sport so fun. He gave tons of feedback to make us all better, and he always seemed like he was having fun and like there was nowhere he'd rather be than with our team. I was so motivated that

CLIMATE IN ACTION 8.2 Continued

season to work on my skills and develop as a player. Wendel, unfortunately for me and my teammates, got a job at a college the next year and moved away. If I'd had volleyball coaches like him after that, I'd still be playing the sport. Looking back, I'm glad I had him for that year. I saw how much fun a volleyball season could be when athletes have a coach like Wendel.

Shared by Lindsey Fry

Note: Wendel Camargo is an Assistant Volleyball Coach at Texas A&M University

---

- **Do team building activities.** There are many fun team building activities to do and ideas for these kinds of activities are readily available in books and on the internet. Activities as simple as keeping multiple beach balls in the air for a certain count (without hitting the ground), marching in a line with balloons scrunched in between each person (athletes can't touch the balloons with their hands/arms), and playing hacky sack (to get a team record for touches) are simple activities that can help athletes bond as a team, if done in a supportive manner. Some teams might live near a ropes course and could have an opportunity to do something on a bigger level that could be important for the group.
- **Change the pace.** Coaches might think of activities to do outside their sport that could be fun, like trying frisbee golf at a local park, taking a morning to canoe or go for a hike at a nearby lake or park, bowling, or playing putt-putt. Coaches would not even have to make these big outside events; they could even throw a nerf football or frisbee around after practice just to have a change of pace. They can also change the pace within practice by deciding to play a different sport or give athletes choices. Today you can go for a run in the park, play sand volleyball, or have a fun game of wiffle ball.
- **Build in rest and recovery time.** For both coaches and athletes, as the season progresses, it can become a grind. Trying to balance school, sport, family and friends can be grueling, and having days off can be just what the team needs. Some coaches give an occasional day off and encourage athletes to take a nap, spend time doing something they haven't had time to do, reconnect with family and friends, or whatever they feel they need to recharge their batteries. Some coaches find it most helpful to let athletes know that in the next two weeks they are allowed to pick one day to take off from practice. The advantage is that athletes can plan for the day and choose a time when they feel it will especially benefit them. An added benefit is that athletes really feel they have a choice in the matter. The downside of this approach is that

it may not allow for coaches to have a day off (which may be a critical piece of the puzzle), although if there are multiple coaches on a team this could still work.

- **Talk about grit in the toughest period of the season.** In Chapter 4 we discussed how special it is when a team sticks together across an entire season and, regardless of their record, has athletes that are all-in. As the season progresses and everyone begins to feel more fatigue, it's a great time to have conversations about how sport can parallel life. Coach Darren Erpelding says he is intentional about talking to his team about adversity. He wants the lesson of grit to transcend their sport season. He says he asks his athletes, "If we don't quit when things get tough in soccer, why the heck would we quit when they get tough in life?" Conversations like this help athletes give meaning to their perseverance and their ability to get through challenging times as people, and as teammates who help one another.

- **Pass around responsibility.** Another way athletes can be given opportunities to get to know one another is to be given responsibility for tasks. A coach might say, "*Katy & Randi, I'd like you two to lead the warm-up for tomorrow's practice. You two pick the stretches and activities we do and the music. Can you two work as a team to do that together? Awesome, you rock! Can't wait for tomorrow!*"

- **Encourage connections among athletes.** Coaches could set up a schedule where they pair athletes up to connect for brief meetings throughout the season. It is the athletes' responsibility to figure out when to meet and perhaps what to talk about (or the coach could give some direction, if needed), but basically the coach would be encouraging teammates to intentionally make connections with others on the team. If more teams did this there would likely be fewer misjudgments, misunderstandings, and assumptions made about teammates because they would be speaking directly to one another.

- **Tune in to athletes' lives outside of sport.** Some coaches are good about knowing the other activities their athletes are involved in and it can be fun for the team to recognize and support these. For example, a coach might say at the end of practice, "*I can't wait to see Kiira and Sami in the play this weekend*" or "*Derby, Betty, and Virginia, I'm looking forward to hearing how the Scholar Bowl team performs at Saturday's competition*," or "*I'm excited about Isabel's quinceañera this weekend.*" Noting the worthwhile activities athletes are involved in is nice for both the athletes and their teammates, as it recognizes young people for more than just their sport accomplishments.

- **Seek athletes' help in improving drills.** Coaches should strive to make drills fun as athletes give high effort and are so much more engaged when they enjoy what they are doing. One idea coaches could try is to do a drill, and then put athletes in groups of three or so and give them 3 minutes to brainstorm ideas about how to improve the drill in terms of maximizing participation, time, fun, and skill development. Coaches might also give their athletes the challenge of designing a drill for a certain purpose (e.g., working on getting the ball down the court faster, serving and volleying, turning double plays, etc.). Coaches may be surprised that even young athletes can have great ideas for drills that would help the team, in addition to improving drills the team may already know.

- **Keep the focus on your athletes.** In the Climate in Action 8.3, Chelsi Scott.describes a high school coach that had the radar zoned in on what was best for Chelsi, from inviting her to go out for cross country in her freshman year, to adding fun events throughout the season, to facilitating her recovery from injury. Coaches like Mary Ellen Stronant leave an indelible mark on their athletes.

CLIMATE IN ACTION 8.3

As a basketball player, running was more a form of conditioning rather than a sport. However, the spring before entering high school, the girls' cross country coach approached me at a track meet to discuss my potential on the team. In that conversation, my future coach explained to me the type of athletes she wanted on her team: athletes who were hard working, dedicated and above all, team players. She said she had a great relationship with my basketball coach and knew that if I put in the effort to practice my running, I could have a great high school running career. As it turns out, my running career was quite short of stunning. However, Coach Stronant never made me feel anything less than an equal on the team. Although only the top seven runners score in cross country meets, Coach Stronant coached each team member as if they alone impacted the team. Throughout my four years of running cross country, she was nothing less than supportive, encouraging and above all loving. In practice, she provided a beautiful combination of tailored, technical instruction mixed with positive and motivating encouragement for each athlete, regardless of their ability. Outside of practice, she hosted barbeques and movie nights, she took us to running clinics to help improve our form and even searched for the best deals on running gear to help those of us who struggled paying for new running shoes every season to afford proper attire. Mary Ellen was more than a coach, she was a second mom, a role model and above all, a kind person. Nothing epitomizes this more than when, in my senior year, I found out I had developed a pretty severe stress fracture half-way through our fall season. Knowing that basketball was my primary sport and the sport I was pursuing to play collegiately, Coach Stornant did not hesitate "benching" me for the season so that I could

CLIMATE IN ACTION 8.3 Continued

heal. While she expressed her sadness that I would be unable to compete, especially with our team being unusually small that season, she reiterated that being healthy for basketball season was more important at that time in my life. Beyond her compassion with the injury itself, she understood how much being a part of the team meant to me. So, when I was cleared to engage in non-running activities, Coach Stornant offered up her bike for me to ride along with the team as they ran. Sometimes she even allowed me to rollerblade with the team so she could ride along. She also included me in practice planning and race-day operations, still allowing me to serve as captain and lead my team despite my injury. By the time basketball season came around, not only was I healed, but I also was conditioned enough to begin practice at full strength. In my four years with Coach Stornant, not only did I become a better athlete, but also a better person, and for that I will always be grateful.

Shared by Chelsi Scott

- **Regulate your emotions.** Seasons can be long, and it's easy for coaches to suffer from fatigue and respond with ups and downs in their ability to bring energy to the team. In the Climate in Action, 8.4, Matt Bragga, Rice University's head baseball coach, reflects on a lesson he learned during his days as an assistant coach about the importance of consistency. How can coaches expect athletes to demonstrate maturity and emotional control if the coaches take their team on a daily emotional rollercoaster? It is not common to observe coaches deal with this issue, but what a gift to athletes when they can display a high quality of emotional regulation across the season. They might be helping athletes in important ways also learn to control the emotional highs and lows that are characteristic of adolescence.

CLIMATE IN ACTION 8.4

I learned from Brian [Coach Shoop] that even though the season can have ups and downs and be a grind at times, you can still be the same person everyday, very consistent and steady. That's all a player can ask, is for a coach to be consistent. I don't think the players respond well to a coach who is a Jekyll-and-Hyde, up one day, down the next. When coaches are all fired up one day and the next they are down, yelling and angry, it's tough for a player to know how to respond to that. I was like that at Bevill State, but because of Coach Shoop's influence, I learned to be a little more consistent.[1]

Shared by Coach Matt Bragga [Rice University head baseball coach]

- **Make things better**. Coaches might also think about activities their teams could do for others in their school or community. Joe Ehrmann, former collegiate and NFL player, describes how his high school football team had a rule that they did not allow any student to eat alone in the cafeteria.[2] The football players, when they entered the cafeteria with their lunches, were trained to look around the room, and if a student was sitting alone, they joined that student's table. The idea is that it is no fun not having someone to sit with at lunch, and the team being aware of this is one strategy they can use to make their school a better place for all students. What a fun idea to have athletes think about how, as a collective force, they could work together to make things better. Maybe they help an older person in their community by raking leaves in their yard or other chores around the house, or provide items for a family in need, or plan and put on a free sport clinic for children in their community or area that could benefit, or write letters of support to peers who are in a juvenile facility or hospital ward. There are so many ways that teams can work together to build a caring and task-involving climate on their teams and carry the spirit out to others.
- **Reinforce that opponents are not enemies**. Early in the season, it is also key for coaches to reinforce for athletes the notion that their opponents are not enemies. They should understand that sport is so much more fun when they have strong opponents who care deeply about the sport and give their best effort. As a result, opponents should be held in high regard with the utmost respect. In different circumstances, their opponents might be best friends, but in any circumstances, the potential is there to build relationships with opponents and this should be encouraged. One way coaches do this is to make the effort to have positive interactions with other coaches and their athletes and to encourage their athletes to do the same.
- **Keep the feedback coming.** As the season progresses, it is easy for coaches to let up on the amount of feedback they give some of their athletes. One of the things that athletes want the most from their coach, is feedback to help them continue to improve their skills. In Climate in Action, 8.5 Jamee McGinnes describes his high school track coach who kept giving him feedback and encouragement across the season, and how much that meant to his continued development as an athlete.

CLIMATE IN ACTION 8.5

When I was in high school, my track and field head coach [Phil Katzenmeier] really helped me stay positive about my performance no matter what the result. Even though he was primarily a sprints and middle six range coach, he would always take the time to come watch the throwing events and give insight on how to improve form, even though his other athletes may have

---

CLIMATE IN ACTION 8.5 Continued

been running. If I was ever discouraged after a performance, he noticed and made sure he talked to me about it and assured me that there was always a new day to get better and put the negatives in the past and focus on the future. His positive talks and actions really helped improve my performance and the morale of all my teammates around me. I am truly grateful for Coach Katzenmeier and all he did for my development as a student athlete.

Shared by Jamison McGinness

In different ways, these strategies can contribute to enhancing the features of a caring and task-involving climate throughout the season. Some might be more effective for emphasizing the caring dimension of the team while others might give athletes an opportunity to see the great qualities in their teammates. Others might foster cooperation. It is fun for coaches to think about how they can zoom in on the features, design activities that will result in the overall creation of a caring and task-involving climate on their teams.

Activities to End the Season with a Caring and Task-involving Climate

Carrying through with an emphasis on creating a caring and task-involving climate at the end of the season is key. We observe many teams finish with a strong ego-involving end of the year event. What we mean by this is that coaches might award "Most Valuable Athlete" awards, highlight how some athletes out-performed others, and put the spotlight only on performance outcomes. We have observed coaches using a basketball metric that takes a lot of information (for example, points scored, minutes played, etc.) and the software program calculates a number that represents each athlete's contribution to the team. One athlete's score is a 15.6 and another is a 2.4. Highlighting this kind of information is distracting. The audience of parents and athletes are likely unclear what the number means, and it suggests that some athletes were extremely important to the team whereas others might even have been a burden. We are impressed when we see coaches use the end of year event to reinforce the team's overall commitment to developing their skills, supporting one another, playing the game in a respectful manner, and celebrating each person's contribution to the team. Contrast the following two coaches' approach to their team's end of year picnic:

- **Team 1 (The Rams).** *"Thanks everyone for coming tonight. We're ready to start the awards part of our banquet. The first award is the Most Improved and it goes to a person who has worked really hard this season. He wasn't one of our top scorers or* *anything, but he worked hard every day and we just saw a lot of improvement in him across the season. This award goes to Troy (lots of applause). The next award is the Hardest Worker Award and it goes to a person that just never gave up, no matter what the situation with our team. This athlete never leaves anything on the court, whether it's a practice or competition, and this award goes to Bernie (lots of applause). The next award is our Most Valuable Player Award. It's sort of self-explanatory, but this athlete was really key to our success this season. This award goes to Gary (lots of applause). Well, there is more food left, so feel free to stay longer, but thanks for coming. Oh, yes, and we'd like our award winners to stay for pictures."*

The coaches might continue with a few more awards (Outstanding Defensive/Offensive Player) but at the end of the day, only a few athletes are typically acknowledged, and in a caring and task-involving climate, this is not the aim. Hopefully every athlete was deserving of the effort and most improved awards, for example, and it puts a damper on the evening to just hear about the contribution of several athletes to the team. When we really think about it, it seems messed up that this tradition ever got started, but we are so used to seeing this approach in sport that it has become the norm. Contrast this approach in comparison to the Hawks.

- **Team 2 (The Hawks).** *"I want to welcome everyone to our end of the year picnic. I am glad that we can come together as a team and celebrate the season we've had. Personally, I've had a blast getting to work with all these young athletes, and seeing their improvement across the season, their determination to hang in there each competition, and work together to be the best we could be. We're very fortunate to have such great parents [of the athletes] who have supported this team in so many big and small ways. The team talked about what we wanted to do tonight to celebrate the season and this is what the athletes came up with …"*
  - o *"The athletes decided they wanted to each get up and say a few words about one of their teammates, and offer their perspective about what the athlete contributed and why she was an important part of our season. So, we're going to start with Virginia, introducing Ali."*
  - o *"The athletes decided they wanted to each share a favorite memory they have of playing on this team this year. I think we have so many great memories that we will take with us, and I thought the athletes had a great idea with this, so we're going to start with Joe."*

The ideas are endless for how to wrap up a season in a fun way that recognizes each athlete, rather than a few at the expense of the rest of the team. What if coaches shared special moments about each athlete, or what if each athlete had a chance to share what they learned from being part of the team or what about being on the team made them a better person?

Someone (coaches, parents, athletes) might put together a fun slideshow of pictures from across the season. Everyone could be invited to take and share these pictures across the season. It might be fun to get pictures of athletes posing with special family members and friends that came to watch games, younger siblings who played together while the games were going on, officials, etc. These are just a few ideas, but the point is that in a caring and task-involving climate, an end-of-season celebration should be fun and inclusive of all athletes.

*****

The key to creating a caring and task-involving climate is to start at the very beginning of the season from the first day, and reinforce the features of the climate every day thereafter. Together, coaches, athletes, and parents can unite in their buy-in of the value of creating a caring and task-involving climate, and their commitment to making it happen.

Reflecting on Practice

Coaches must be intentional about creating a caring and task-involving climate with their teams, and this takes planning. We suggest that coaches reflect on the five features of the climate, and first summarize the kinds of things they currently do to bring out the features. It's likely that coaches are already doing many things highlighted in this chapter. Focusing on what they are doing now can help coaches identify some of their stronger areas as well as areas that could be strengthened.

- What am I currently doing to bring the five features to life on my team?
  - ❏ Everyone is treated with mutual kindness and respect.
  - ❏ Effort and Improvement are valued and recognized.
  - ❏ Mistakes are part of learning.
  - ❏ Everyone plays an important role.
  - ❏ Cooperation among teammates is fostered.
- What do I think I'm doing well?
- What are areas where I can further enhance the climate? What ideas do I have for new activities or strategies that will bring the five features of a caring and task-involving climate to life?
- What can I do to insure that I'm still creating a strong caring and task-involving climate as the season progresses?

Communities of Practice

It might be fun and interesting to read this chapter with your coaching staff and brainstorm together how you could utilize ideas and keep one another accountable across the season to have a strong caring and task-involving climate on the team.

Sources

1 Madison, K. (2019). Matt Bragga: Havin' fun and gettin' it done. *Inside Pitch*, March/April, 18–20.
2 Ehrmann, J. (2011). *Inside-out coaching: How sports can transform lives.* New York: Simon and Schuster.

9

EXPERIENCING A CARING AND TASK-INVOLVING CLIMATE

Who Benefits Most?

Highlights

- Every young athlete benefits from experiencing a caring and task-involving climate.
- A caring and task-involving climate may be especially important for some young athletes.

As has been outlined in the book to this point, we believe that young athletes benefit from experiencing a caring and task-involving climate. For so many reasons that have been emphasized already, a caring and task-involving climate allows all athletes to be in a safe setting where they can learn, develop, feel connected, and be given the resources to help maximize their sport experience and their performance. Even though a caring and task-involving climate is good for all young people, in this chapter we highlight circumstances where particular athletes might experience a boost in terms of the positive effects they receive. For a myriad of reasons, it may be especially impactful for certain athletes to reap the benefits of an environment where the features of a caring and task-involving climate are heightened. We will highlight some of these athletes now.

- **Low skilled**. Athletes who have had less exposure to sport and physical activity and who may be lagging in their development of sport knowledge and skills may feel like they hit the lottery when they find themselves in a caring and task-involving climate. Because coaches are focused on helping every athlete keep the focus on their personal effort and improvement, rather than hyping the best athletes on the team, low skilled athletes will be more likely to work towards their athletic potential. In a caring and task-involving climate, every athlete is receiving feedback to help them improve, and are reminded that giving high effort is the meter by which the team gauges their success. Because all athletes on the team, not just the most gifted and best performers, are receiving encouragement for their efforts, low skilled athletes are less likely to feel discouraged and more likely to feel that their involvement is fun and meaningful.

- **Late bloomers.** So often in youth sport, children need time to develop, but if they find themselves in ego-involving climates where the emphasis is primarily on winning, they may be relegated to the bench and receive little feedback and less playing time than their peers. In a task-involving climate, coaches give everyone playing time so that all athletes have real opportunities to learn and improve in both practice and competitions. If late bloomers do not get opportunities to grow and develop early on in their sport involvement, they will likely be youth that see no fun in sport and give it up early. Our society has much to gain from helping all young people have a positive sport experience. They are more likely to stick with sport, and definitely more likely to be physically active as they move through life. A side note is that many great athletes were late bloomers, including Michael Jordan, who was cut from his high school basketball team. Coaches miss out on working with talented athletes when they do not understand that late bloomers bloom bright when the time is right, but only when they have had the opportunity to grow and develop in caring and task-involving climates.

- **Youth with a different physical stature.** Sometimes children who are smaller, and less developed physically are at a disadvantage in youth sport, but this is not the case when coaches create a caring and task-involving climate. Children in this environment are made to feel valued and welcome, rather than self-conscious and inferior. They are given opportunities to develop their sport skills in a fun and stimulating environment where they are not teased for being smaller than others. It can also be the case that sometimes children who are larger have a more difficult time in youth sport. This can occur, for example, in gymnastics, diving, and dance, where a smaller physique is sometimes preferred. In these cases, children with a larger frame may feel at a disadvantage, out of place, and like all eyes are on them. These feelings can be especially rough for girls, who receive more pressure from society to fit the tall and slim model that is favored in the U.S. In a caring and task-involving climate, coaches intentionally work to make larger children feel as if they belong and are important members of the group. Regardless of young athletes' physiques, they are all provided a positive and supportive environment when the coach reinforces the features of a caring and task-involving climate.

- **Youth with health issues.** In a caring and task-involving climate, coaches are committed to caring about each athlete, and providing support for those who have special needs. Children who have asthma, diabetes, ADHD and other physical and mental health conditions, are seen as valuable members of the team, and not as liabilities that get in the way of the team winning. Coaches who create a caring and task-involving climate, use health issues as important occasions for teaching children about the specifics of having these conditions and diseases. Though health issues may place limitations on young people's participation in some ways, they rarely prevent them from playing the sport, and many times with very few restrictions. It is unfortunate when coaches and administrators are uninformed about health issues and make them a bigger deal for athletes than they are. Coaches who are not working hard to create a caring and task-involving climate do a disservice to young athletes who could be reaping many benefits from sport but may be held out due to a lack of knowledge on the part of coaches. Seattle Seahawk Shaquem Griffin is a linebacker playing in the NFL. When he was four years old he suffered from amniotic band syndrome, a condition that cost him part of one of his arms.[1] Rebekkah Gregory, who lost a leg in the Boston Marathon bombing in 2013, went on to complete the race two years later.[2] The list of athletes is long that have overcome physical and cognitive challenges to join their peers in playing sports that they love, and that help them grow and develop as both athletes and people. It is powerful when coaches see the potential in every one of their athletes, despite the physical and mental challenges they face.

- **Athletes who have fewer opportunities to participate in physical activity or positive youth development programs.** Some children have minimal opportunities to participate in out of school programs that include physical activity and positive development. They have had less exposure to sport, and when they do have chance to be in a sport program, it is important for them to be able to experience a caring and task-involving climate.

CLIMATE IN ACTION 9.1

American Indian Youth. We have been involved with helping to train coaches on the Zuni Reservation in Zuni, NM to create a caring and task-involving climate within their youth sport programs, and coaches have been very receptive to implementing this approach. The historical poor treatment of American Indians in the U.S. has resulted in long-term problems on reservations that include a lack of financial resources, proper medical care, employment opportunities, effective schools, and rich activities for children outside the school day. Clearly, many American Indian Youth grow up on reservations where they are not given every opportunity to thrive and to make the most of their gifts and abilities. The volunteer coaches in the Zuni Youth Enrichment Program understand the importance of helping children have a positive youth sport experience where they make physical, social, and cognitive gains in their development.

Shared by the KU Sport & Exercise Psychology Lab

CLIMATE IN ACTION 9.2

Strong Girls. We have run a program for elementary school girls in our community called Strong Girls that was focused on providing both physical and positive youth development activities, delivered again within a caring and task-involving framework. Female college students volunteered as mentors to these girls that came to our college campus each week after school for a session. Over the years this program ran, we had incredible results where girls reported feeling more confident to try new activities, less worried about how they compared to others, and more focused on giving their best effort and letting everything else take care of itself. During a panel where we took some of the participants to a conference, an audience member asked what was the biggest thing the girls got from being a Strong Girl. One said she didn't have test anxiety anymore. She used to get so worried and upset about every exam at school, and at Strong Girls she learned to go in to a test, do the best she could on that day, and get ready for the next day. Another child said she had felt much stress and anxiety due to the huge success of her older sibling who received national recognition at a young age for his accomplishments. She felt she needed to follow in his footsteps even though the activity he pursued did not align with her passion. She described how Strong Girls helped her learn to walk her own path, and to create her own dreams. We chalk up the successes experienced in the Strong Girls program to the foundation of the program which was the creation of a caring and task-involving climate.

Shared by the KU Sport & Exercise Psychology Lab

- **Athletes who are part of military families or families that relocate often.** Some children are part of families that relocate often, and this can make it challenging for them to build and sustain relationships. These athletes may find themselves being the 'new kid on the block' every time they turn around. In a caring and task-involving climate, coaches recognize that special care should be taken to be welcoming to such athletes, and to help them connect and feel the support of their teammates. If athletes are part of military families, coaches' awareness of parents that may be stationed away from home can be especially important. Parents who are serving the country in this capacity, often have children that do not have the luxury of having parents available to attend their games and support them directly in other team activities.

- **Young athletes who experience injuries.** Sometimes young athletes experience injuries that cause them to miss out on practices and games. Injuries can be frustrating because athletes can feel disconnected from their coaches and teammates, and wonder what role they will play on the team when they return. In a caring and task-involving climate, coaches help athletes support one another during times of injury. Coaches are sensitive and feel empathy for injured athletes, and they look for ways to reassure athletes and keep the connections with them strong.

- **Youth with low social support.** We live in a world where too many children come out on the short end of receiving social support from family and friends. Some children do not have caring adults in their corner who are looking out for their best interests, and in these cases, coaches play an extra important role in creating a caring and task-involving climate for young athletes. Sadly, the only exposure some youngsters have to authentic and unconditional support may come from their sport involvement, and in particular having a coach that gets to know them on a personal level, conveys a deep sense of caring for their well-being, and provides that family atmosphere through the creation of a caring and task-involving climate.

- **Youth who have challenging lives.** Many families have a lot going on behind the scenes that make children's lives challenging. We know families who are struggling with financial issues, stress from their jobs, health issues within their primary family or extended family (aging grandparents), relationship issues between parents or parents and their children, etc. It is easy to think of childhood as a care-free period where all is bliss, but the reality is that many children are dealing with difficult situations within their families. It is not unusual for coaches to have athletes that have experienced trauma during their childhood. In a caring and task-involving climate, coaches help children have fun, develop relationships, engage in physical activity, strengthen their sport skills, and perhaps provide a distraction from the stresses they are dealing with outside of sport. Coaches also help children learn to focus on things they can control, build resilient mindsets, and know that they are surrounded by coaches and teammates that support them. All of these serve to help children live healthier and happier lives. How unfortunate for children who find themselves in ego-involving sport climates where winning is the primary aim, and where coaches do not take the time or have interest in knowing about them and even more so helping young athletes manage the challenges of their lives.

CLIMATE IN ACTION 9.3

Young People Involved in the Juvenile Justice System. We have also conducted work with young residents of the state Juvenile Correctional Complex, which is a high security facility (prison) for youngsters under the age of 18 years. We have provided workshops focused on positive life skills and physical activity, and delivered them within a caring and task-involving climate. College students served as mentors in the program, and shared

CLIMATE IN ACTION 9.3 Continued

their initial trepidation that the youth might not respond favorably to the sessions. The expectation from some was that the youth might think the activities we planned were stupid, childish, and beneath them. They also were wondering if the youth would be rude, disrespectful, and whether they would feel a sense of fear that the youth would react in a violent way. After all, these youth are in a high-security facility for many reasons. What we found surprised our college helpers. The youth at the facility were warm, friendly, and very appreciative of our sessions. They soaked up being in a caring environment, where they were treated with kindness and respect, encouraged to participate fully, and could feel safe around our group. They even shared much more than our group anticipated through each of the activities. The lesson was huge for our college student volunteers, some of whom were expecting the worse from these young people. So much of what is portrayed through television and the media make it seem as if individuals incarcerated in our prisons need tough love, and that it's good for them to live in bare circumstances where they have plenty of time to reflect on their misdeeds. Some in the popular press would say we should not coddle individuals who committed crimes, we don't need to provide a rich and welcoming environment, and we don't need to help them feel safe enough to develop meaningful relationships in their lives. Our work has reinforced our belief that 1) Experiencing a caring climate is key for every human being, and 2) Individuals who make mistakes need to be treated with kindness and respect, and helped to build a new life where they can channel their skills and gifts in a positive direction.

Shared by the KU Sport & Exercise Psychology Lab

- **Youth who live in areas where safety is an issue.** Many children in the U.S. and around the globe live in places where there exist high levels of crime and a disregard for the welfare of others. Sport programs that manifest a caring and task-involving climate play a critical role for youth who live in such circumstances. Such a sport climate provides a rich resource that helps with community building. If children can participate on a team where they are taught to treat others with kindness and respect, and experience the joy that comes in developing a passion to be the best that they can be, they may take these skills back to their families, schools, and communities, and make them better. We have frequently had parents share with us their observations that their children come home and teach the fundamental principles of creating a caring and task-involving climate to their siblings. How cool is that?!

CLIMATE IN ACTION 9.4

Children in Guatemala. We have partnered with Children International to help with their Game On program that provides physical activity programming to youth living in poor areas across the globe. We provided training to their volunteer coaches, many of whom are former youth in the program and/or parents of youth in the program. These volunteers care about children and want to help, but most lack training in education and child development. Through a weekend workshop we were able to help these caring adults see how they could create a caring and task-involving climate within their program. An amazing finale to this work occurred when we were able to visit their specific program sites to see their implementation of strategies to help create a caring and task-involving climate. We've never had so much fun as we had watching these programs provide powerful and transformational opportunities to children in the community to come and experience such a caring and task-involving environment. Our work in Guatemala brought home the idea that this climate is universally beneficial.

Shared by the KU Sport & Exercise Psychology Lab

*****

Our work has led us to interact with many groups who have implemented a caring and task-involving climate in their programs, and we wanted, in this chapter, to note a few of these groups. We believe in the power of creating a caring and task-involving climate and we love seeing how helpful it can be to a wide variety of young athletes. In summary, a caring and task-involving climate is HUGE for all young people. The features that help children see the joy that comes from working hard, seeing self-improvement, learning to cooperate with others, approaching mistakes as opportunities for learning, and learning to treat all individuals with kindness and respect are effective guides for having productive and meaningful lives.

Reflecting on Practice

Coaches can benefit from reflecting on athletes they work with who might especially benefit from a caring and task-involving climate. A number of activities and strategies are presented in this book to highlight how to create such a positive climate. Coaches can reflect on the following questions, thinking in particular about those young athletes who would especially benefit from a caring and task-involving climate.

- What are my reactions to the information presented in this chapter? What ideas did the information prompt me to think about?
- What athletes have I worked with that have reaped particular benefits of their exposure to a caring and task-involving climate? What were those benefits?
- Which current athletes may benefit most from being in a caring and task-involving climate? Which former athletes particularly benefited from being in a caring and task-involving climate?
- What strategies can I try that are suggested in this book to support those athletes I identified?

Sources

[1]   Tears as one-handed Shaquem Griffin joins twin brother in NFL for Seahawks. Retrieved April 21, 2019 from the *Guardian*: www.theguardian.com/sport/2018/apr/28/shaquem-griffin-nfl-draft-seattle-seahawks

[2]   Rosenbaum, S. (2015). Woman who lost leg in Boston Marathon bombing finishes this year's race. Retrieved April 21, 2019 from the *New York Post*: https://nypost.com/2015/04/21/woman-who-lost-leg-in-boston-marathon-bombing-finishes-this-years-race/

10

OVERCOMING THE CHALLENGES OF CREATING A CARING AND TASK-INVOLVING CLIMATE

Highlights

- Coaches can challenge misperceptions of what it means to create a caring and task-involving climate.
- Coaches can navigate playing time issues within the context of a caring and task-involving climate.
- Coaches can manage behavioral problems within the context of a caring and task-involving climate.
- Coaches can work with athletes who exhibit low commitment.
- Coaches can help when athletes share difficult personal experiences.
- Coaches can maintain their own effort and energy.

We believe that most coaches engage in the profession and practice from a place of "care" because they want to be involved in young athletes' lives. These coaches are genuinely interested in the process of developing athletes' sport and life skills and they do not see coaching as a means to an end, that is, focus just on winning. We believe that creating a caring and task-involving climate is aligned with this coaching philosophy. However, we recognize that there may be some challenges and roadblocks to creating a caring and task-involving climate. In this chapter, we consider a variety of common obstacles that coaches can encounter and provide resources and strategies to surmount them.

When People Believe that a Caring and Task-Involving Climate is in Opposition to Winning

For a variety of reasons, some people may believe that winning is the most important goal of youth sports. Therefore, when they hear coaches talking about a caring and task-involving climate they may comment, *"What does this have to do with sport? Aren't we here to just let them play and learn how to compete and win?"* Others might perhaps say, *"Isn't this just making people soft and not preparing them for the cut-throat environment of competition? You should really be spending more time toughening them up and preparing them for the real world reality that there are winners and losers."* In these instances, coaches need to remind people that creating a caring and task-involving climate is a winning combination. Here are some sample comments coaches can use to refute those ideas:

- *"Emphasizing effort, improvement, learning from mistakes, and working together to reach a common goal are essential components in putting together a winning team. In fact, how great is it that I do not have to yell, demean, or punish my players but yet each athlete is continuing to improve on this team."*
- *"Setting high expectations and challenging members of this team is critical to winning. However, it is much easier to hold athletes accountable to these expectations in a system that focuses on those things they can control, their effort, and where I and their teammates are supporting them to achieve their goals rather than pitting them against one another. I get more out of my athletes when creating a caring and task-involving climate and that means we are more successful."*
- *"Competition is an important part of this program and is essential to creating a caring and task-involving climate. During a competitive event, our opponent challenges us and provides an opportunity to see our true skill level. They give us insight into where we excel and where we need to improve. It is thrilling and fun to be challenged in this way. This is a gift and as such we should treat our opponent with respect and look forward to each competition."*
- *"Creating a caring and task-involving climate is not easy and it does not make kids weak. We have high expectations for our athletes, we have intense and effortful practice, and we excel. All while being caring, it certainly does not sound soft to me."*
- *"Our program emphasizes performance excellence but not at the expense of teaching life skills. Your child's experience in sport is temporary but the life lessons, like learning to overcome adversity by learning from mistakes, learning to treat others with kindness and value their contribution, and striving to be better in everything they do, I hope will last a lifetime."*
- *"Competing and coming to understand how one compares to others provides important information that will help our team be successful. However, on this team we do not make that center stage. Rather, we use that information to help us improve. This improvement comes when we focus on the things we can control, like our effort, personal improvement, and learning from mistakes. Plus, we seek to support one another because success in life is about working together and reaching our potential."*

When Playing Time Issues Arise

Many coaches have had to address parents who have concerns that their child is not getting enough playing time. In fact, parents and athletes may accuse the coach of not caring about the athlete. There are several considerations to make in responding to this concern that align with a caring and task-involving climate. Here are a few:

- First, coaches want to understand the specific concern. For example, if the parent is concerned that the child is not making progress in the sport, the coach can use it as an opportunity to discuss how the child has progressed and show the parents assessments the coach has made. The key here is that coaches need to be monitoring progress and improvement (as noted in Chapter 4). Alternatively, if the parent is concerned that the child is not competing enough to prepare for the next team level (for example, moving to travel ball), the coach can discuss how developing strong fundamentals in practice sessions rather than in competition is more critical to moving to the next level. Therefore, to really help their child improve suggest additional practice time. This practice time may perhaps be accomplished by providing parents ideas to play some fun activities at home with their child. It will be critical for the coach to help the parents understand what fundamental movements need to be emphasized and that the activities are for play with the parent not the parent as coach.
- As a coach, it is key to share a team and league philosophy that encourages all athletes to get the same playing time as other athletes. This philosophy may have been instituted to make sure that every athlete could test their skills in a competitive environment.
- As a coach, it is important to be honest and genuine regarding the athlete's abilities and what he or she needs to do to improve that could warrant more playing time. While, it is important to not promise playing time to any athlete, as there are several factors that determine playing time, it is important to have a clearly stated policy.

If these alternatives are not perceived amenable to parents, genuinely communicate with empathy and suggest another team the athlete may join that will help the parents and child achieve their goals. Although this is a hard conversation, having it shows care for the athlete (and their parents).

When There is a Need to Correct Behavioral Issues

As all coaches know, there are times in which athletes' misbehave. When athletes do misbehave, coaches are often disappointed and frustrated as they believe that the athletes really do not care. Coaches sometimes forget that young athletes are in need of instruction to foster positive behaviors as well as good role models. While we have already highlighted ways to use developmental discipline to handle misbehaviors from the perspective of mutual respect (see Chapter 3), we feel there are additional strategies coaches can use that align with a caring and task-involving climate. For example, as Rainer Martens notes in his book, *Successful coaching*, coaches correct their athletes' behavior by using a *positive discipline approach* which "views discipline as training that develops self-control in your disciples."[1] Here are some ideas coaches can consider aligned with creating a caring and task-involving climate to proactively and reactively manage athlete behaviors.

Set Clear Expectations

Athletes can benefit from having clear rules for behavior, expectations, and consequences to unacceptable behaviors to enhance athletes' accountability and conflict. Clear expectations will minimize conflict and the occurrence of negative behavior and assure consistency in practice. Coaches may even want to have a comprehensive handbook that includes team values, team expectations, team rules, and associated consequences, to be shared with the team, assistant coaches, and parents.

Foster a Culture of Positive Behavior

From an angle of positive coaching, it is useful to create a culture on your team where positive behavior, work ethic, and respect is expected and rewarded. Nurture a team culture in which holding others accountable and using positive discipline is the norm. Have discussions with the team and analyze the consequences of disregarding team values for the team experience and their goals and have the team weigh in on the conversation. If athletes come to accept and value the culture, they will be more ready to abide by its norms and encourage their teammates to do so as well.

Consider Whether Athletes are Aware of Proper Behavior

Before addressing athletes' misbehavior, coaches may want to consider whether the athletes knew the correct behavior or whether the proper behavior has been explained and taught to the athletes. With the large amount of things that coaches need to teach their athletes, they may sometimes assume that knowing how to respectfully speak to a coach, for example, has already been learned by the athlete, when this may not be the case. Coaches' should teach the behavior. For example, a coach can say, "*Okay guys, while I am explaining a technique or play, I need everybody focusing and listening until I am done. That means all eyes on me and being able to repeat back what I say. Following this you can ask questions. Okay?*" Then the coach can provide opportunities to practice, and finally correct it when needed. For instance, "*Hey Robert, you know that you should not interrupt until I am done explaining, just hold your thought until I am done and then you can raise your hand and ask the question.*"

When Athletes Purposefully Misbehave

When athletes purposefully misbehave, coaches need to promptly correct the behavior. However, coaches may easily get frustrated when this occurs and not act from a place of care or personal improvement. Therefore, coaches must remind themselves of their intention to create a caring and task-involving climate. Within this climate, a coach can constructively teach the athlete the proper behavior with kindness and respect. The coach should be clear, and set limits by communicating with caring and without demeaning the athlete. For example, a coach could say, *"Josh, I understand that you don't like when others block you and you get frustrated, but you can't push your teammates away and curse. We have been through this before, and you know that this is not acceptable behavior on this team."*

Additionally, it is important to understand why an athlete may be purposefully misbehaving. For instance, the coach could sit down with Josh and ask him why he chose to misbehave. The athlete may have had a bad day or may be dealing with something else at school. Perhaps Josh was frustrated by not being able to master a skill and lost patience and his temper. Understanding the motive will be useful and having him identify the reasoning behind his action will help him develop self-discipline in the future.

Finally, if a coach learns that misbehavior may be related to a trauma experience, this will require additional actions from the coach. Lou Bergholz and his colleagues[2] offer the following recommendations:

- When communicating with the athlete, who has experienced trauma, a coach should remain calm, keep their voice down, and focus on telling the athlete why they are taking the actions they are taking. For example, *"Okay, I see you are upset and I am taking you out of the game so you can cool down. Remember, focus on those things you can control. Tell me what would be the next play we should run on the court? (athlete responds) Why is this a good option against this team? (athlete responds) What will you do the next time that player tries to get you worked up? (athlete responds) Great. Let's take a few deep breaths, watch the play from the side and I will sub you in a few moments."*
- When an outburst occurs, a coach's initial reaction may be to match the athlete's intense emotion. However, for an athlete that has experienced trauma this may not be helpful. Therefore, after the outburst and the athlete has calmed down, ask the athlete to review what happened in the situation trying to determine what triggered the event and how to act differently the next time it occurs. Regardless, it is very important to have clear behavioral expectations and consequences when they are violated. Therefore, a behavioral consequence, such as taking a timeout from competition, may occur at the point of the outburst until the athlete has calmed down. However, as noted before it is important to have a clearly stated policy of behavioral expectations and consequences.

- When a situation triggers stress for an athlete who has experienced trauma, consider offering opportunities for the athlete to opt out and opt in during practice and competitions. For instance, when an athlete recognizes that their bad stress is occurring they can send you a signal on the bench and you can provide a substitution so the athlete can take a break on the bench until ready to go back into the game.
- As a coach gets to know an athlete and what triggers stress and potential poor behavior on the part of the athlete due to former trauma, help the athlete learn to reframe the situation. A coach might say to an athlete who is falling apart during a game and yelling at her teammates, "*Remember everything is not unraveling, the team just had a couple of mistakes. What do we say?* (athlete responds) *Yes, focus on our successes. Monica had a great rebound, Jess had a strong pass inside and you read the defense well on that last play. You can do this and remember your athletes need your support.*"

When Athletes' Commitment is Low

All coaches want athletes who display motivation by working hard, staying late until they master a skill, and challenging themselves. They also want athletes who exhibit ownership by showing initiative (for example, *Hey coach, should I put the goals out and bring plenty of balls so we can practice shoot outs?*), being self-directed, and helping the coach and team to achieve the team goals. These characteristics represent a strong commitment to the team. However, many coaches have had experiences with athletes who show low commitment to their sport and their team. While sometimes coaches assume players do not care and wonder why they should put all their effort into a team when the athletes do not care, low commitment can come from a variety of sources. In reality, most athletes do care and want to give their best effort and commit to the team but they either have some challenges in their lives or they do not know how to exhibit commitment. An athlete might need to help out at home, work to help support the family, experience some conflict at home, or be struggling in classes. A good place to start is talking to the athlete. Creating a caring connection can start the coach and athlete on a path to figuring out a positive path forward. Often times, by getting to know what is going on in an athlete's life a coach can discern what might be holding the athlete back and provide suggestions for moving forward. Change does not occur overnight so patience and showing an athlete continued respect and kindness is key. In addition to starting from a place of understanding, it may be helpful to consider the following strategies for further enhancing commitment.

Develop a Common Goal

An essential aspect to having a committed team is to make sure athletes understand and buy into the team goals and objectives. If coaches achieve this, they will have a team wanting to do what is needed to succeed. In other words, coaches and athletes need to be "in sync," as a team. An idea to achieve this is to have a team discussion. A coach can have the team sit in a circle in the locker room and ask them to identify the many positive characteristics of the team like, "*Well, we are really good at defense, it is hard for opponents to pass us*" or "*We have Tony and Leo who are so fast they create great advantage.*" The coach can then encourage the team to think about what they need to work on to be an even stronger team. For example, the coach could say, "*Yes! Those are all great examples of things the team does well and we want to capitalize on those strengths this year. So what are we missing? What can do we better this season?*" Coaches may hear things like, "*Well, we get discouraged after a late goal on our side and loose momentum.*" or "*We need to be on the same page on the field and talk to each other more.*" Coaches want to keep writing the athletes ideas on the board and then have the team summarize. For instance, the coach could state, "*It looks like we really need to work on bouncing back and good communication.*" By investing in this discussion and getting to know what they think, athletes may be more likely to commit to these actions throughout the season. However, coaches will need to remind athletes of the goals and keep having these discussions all through the season.

Understand their Commitment Level

In a perfect world, coaches would have highly committed athletes throughout the season. However, the reality is that athletes will display different levels of commitment. To help foster commitment in athletes, coaches can do a quick and practical assessment of commitment. The coach can rate athletes' level of commitment (from low to high) based on their observations in team practices. Once determined, a coach can sit down with the athletes that seem less involved and discuss their commitment level and their goals for the season. This discussion could help the coach understand how to help athletes be more engaged in practices or understand why they really can only give a low level of commitment to the sport.

Recognize that a Lack of Commitment May Actually be Related to Training

People often look at someone with low commitment and think it is related to them personally. However, it may be important for coaches to consider whether the training environment might be the reason that an athlete shows a low level of commitment. For instance, athletes may not seem committed because they are actually tired or fatigued due to the training and practice season and are in need of recovery days. Alternatively, athletes who experience the same routine every day may be exhibiting boredom and could use more variety in their training routine.

When Athletes Share Their Personal Experiences

In developing a caring and task-involving climate, coaches come to know their athletes. Coaches learn about their strengths and weaknesses, their aspirations and hopes, and their successes and struggles. There is great joy in getting to know and share life experiences with athletes as well as being a significant role model to guide and help them develop as people. However, developing a caring and supportive relationship means that athletes will come to trust their coaches and may share traumatic experiences they are facing, like becoming homeless, experiencing physical or sexual abuse, facing deportation of family members, or struggles in relation to mental health. Athletes' willingness to share such experiences with coaches really says something about the type of climate they have created and coaches should feel honored that athletes have chosen them to share these experiences. Yet, these experiences can also create stress for coaches who may not know how to effectively help athletes. Therefore, we believe it is particularly important that caring coaches are aware of resources that can help navigate trauma and mental health issues. Here are a few online resources to learn more information about trauma and mental health issues:

- www.playlikeachampion.org/trauma
- https://appliedsportpsych.org/site/assets/documents/Critical-Incidents-in-Sport.pdf
- www.ncaa.org/sport-science-institute/mind-body-and-sport-mental-health-checklists
- www.thefa.com/~/media/Files/TheFAPortal/governance-docs/equality/disability-and-mental-health/mental-health-awareness-in-sport-resource-pack.ashx
- www.ncaa.org/sport-science-institute/mental-health-educational-resources

Additionally, here are some illustrative conversations to express empathy and also navigate athletes toward appropriate resources.

- ❑ **Trauma example.** *I appreciate that you trusted me enough to tell me about your experience. I cannot even imagine the struggles you have had. How are you managing?* {depending upon response coach can express empathy by reflecting feelings and thoughts and using good active listening skills} [Later in the conversation] *How can I help you?* [After athlete response]. *Here is how I think I can help you* [List ways]. *As I have discussed many times, each of us has strengths and weaknesses that we share with one another but this is an area where I do not have expertise. So while I will support you through this process, let's work together to find experts in this area and additional resources to help.*
- ❑ **Mental health example.** *Thank you for telling me. It can be a difficult journey to live with a mental illness. As you mentioned, I am sure there are days you struggle and other days you are completely fine which can be exhausting and frustrating.* [continuing active listening and respond with empathy] *Just know that I am here*

to support you and if we need to make adjustments in training during a depressive episode, please let me know. Do you currently have a therapist or doctor? [after athlete response collect contact information for emergency situations or if no counselor or doctor provide appropriate resources] *Also, if you are ever thinking about self harm, please let me know. I want the best for you and I want to help. If you are struggling with suicidal thoughts I can connect you with someone who can help.*

Finally, trauma and mental health issues can be all consuming for the athlete and it may require a bit of time and attention on the part of the coach. While it is important to support athletes in their struggle, it is also important to set appropriate boundaries. Here are some considerations:

❑   Coaches should know what they are comfortable doing and what they are not comfortable doing;

❑   Coaches should know when they are required to report incidents to proper authorities (for example, physical abuse);

❑   Coaches should consider their scope of practice and whether they are extending it; and

❑   Coaches should consider whether they are creating a dependency that is unhealthy for either the coach or the athlete.

When it Just Does Not Seem Like it is Worth the Effort

While coaches can see the many positive things that come from creating a caring and task-involving climate, they realize that it requires a lot of work. It requires coaches to plan and be intentional about implementing the features of the climate, it requires time and emotional energy to "be there" for athletes, it requires extra time to communicate the key messages that support this climate, and it requires time to reflect on how it went and ways to improve. This can seem like it adds to the already perceived time crunch felt by many coaches. Coaches may be saying, "*I am being pushed in so many directions! I can't deal with it all.*" The time and effort needed may also mean less time for family, another job, or activities that nurture their own well-being. When there is an imbalance in how coaches spend their time and energy, they may experience fatigued, stress, and dissatisfaction. Under these circumstances coaches may not be able to see that their efforts are making a difference and it is compromising their own life and well-being. While stress is not uncommon, too much stress cannot be sustained and will need to be addressed to prevent burnout. When faced with this challenge, we encourage coaches to consider some of these strategies.

Consider What Work-Life Harmony Looks Like

Coaches may want to consider how much time and effort they give to coaching, family, friends, other jobs, other activities, etc. Coaches will also want to consider how much they want work and life to overlap. If coaches realize that their division of time or the overlap does not match their priorities, they should make adjustments. Coaches may minimize stress from competing tasks between life and work by analyzing their responsibilities, prioritizing them, and reflecting how they manage their time. For example, coaches want to consider whether they are hopping from one task to another and never finishing one? Alternatively, coaches may be "relying on mystical time," which Rainer Martens[3] refers to as time one does not have but may think that one will have later. If so, coaches may want to consider how they can manage their time better and prioritize their life in ways that are meaningful to them and that helps them achieve work-life harmony.

Implement Changes Slowly and Intentionally

We encourage coaches to remember that coaching is about continual improvement so it is okay to make small improvements and do what is manageable to keep work-life harmony. Therefore, coaches should consider slowly and intentionally making changes within their program, including adding the features of the caring and task-involving climate. Further, coaches need to consider whether the new strategies fit into the time and effort they have allotted for coaching. It is not helpful to the coach or team, if the coach is overwhelmed. Chapter 13 will offer a system for being slow and intentional in implementing the climate into practice that coaches may find useful in adapting to other program changes.

Set Up a Support Network

No matter how talented and hard working, none of us, including coaches, are superheroes. And that is okay! It is important that coaches ask for help. Coaches can have a family meeting and explain to them that it has been hard to shuffle everything on practice days and that you feel overworked and stressed. It can sound something like, "*Hey, I know you are all busy too but I wanted to share with you that on practice days I don't seem to get to it all; it is hard to juggle everything at work, home and team practices on Tuesday and Thursday. Matt, I wonder if could get a ride home with Jason, so I don't have to rush and can take some extra time at the team parents' meeting. Kate, if you could tag along with me some days, you may help me get the balls and cones out faster so we can start practice on time and be more focused. It would be great help on those two days.*" More often than not, we may find that when we genuinely communicate and disclose our struggles and what is going on with us those around us are very willing to help. Another strategy coaches can use is to broaden their support system. For example, coaches can have parents help to foster a caring and task-involving climate, have an assistant coach run practices to be able to spend time with family or get a workout in, or bring family members to practice to broaden the family atmosphere on the team.

Monitor Physical and Psychological Health

Coaches cannot be successful and teach important life lessons if their health is compromised. Adopting the philosophy of a caring and task-involving climate means that coaches also take time to engage in self-care and improvement in their own physical and mental well-being.

Keep Perspective and Regain Passion

If coaches think back to the first time they coached they will probably be amazed at the progress they have made in their coaching. They may also remember more clearly why they took up the profession of coaching. It is important for coaches to remember why they are coaching and recognize they are doing great work and making a difference in the lives of young people (even if it is just planting seeds and it is not always recognized by others).

*****

In this chapter we considered the challenges coaches may encounter while trying to implement a caring and task-involving climate in their sport. We discussed a few issues that may arise on their teams, which may require patience and authenticity to address, and brought awareness to the personal stresses coaches may endure while implementing a caring and task-involving climate.

Reflecting on Practice

Consider the challenges you face in implementing or maintaining a caring and task-involving climate and how you might work to meet the challenge in a positive and productive way.

Challenge 1:

_____

_____

_____

_____

Overcoming Challenge 1:

_____

_____

_____

_____

_____

Challenge 2:

_____

_____

_____

_____

_____

Overcoming Challenge 2:

_____

_____

_____

_____

_____

Challenge 3:

_____

_____

_____

_____

_____

Overcoming Challenge 3:

_____

_____

_____

_____

_____

Sources

1 Martens, R. (2012). *Successful coaching*. Champaign, IL: Human Kinetics, [p.126].
2 Bergholz, L., Stafford, E., & D'Andrea, W. (2016). Creating trauma-informed sports programming for traumatized youth: Core principles for an adjunctive therapeutic approach. *Journal of Infant, Child, and Adolescent Psychotherapy, 15*(3), 244–253.
3 Martens, R. (2012). *Successful coaching*. Champaign, IL: Human Kinetics, [p.374].

11

MAKING THE PARENT ROLE FUN AND REWARDING BY CREATING A CARING AND TASK-INVOLVING CLIMATE

Highlights

- Parents play a critical role in helping create a caring and task-involving climate for their young athletes.
- Parents can do many things to help optimize their children's sport experiences.

Parenting is a hard job. Parents want to make the right decisions and support their children, help them make good decisions, and thrive in life, but parents can experience much stress when they have to watch their children go through challenging times. So, while parenting may be one of the most fun and rewarding experiences individuals have in their lives, it also comes with trepidation, stress, and at times shaky confidence.

We recognize that for some children, their primary caretakers will be adults other than parents such as guardians or grandparents. For the purpose of this chapter, we are using the term parents to be inclusive of all adult caretakers of youth.

Identify Positive Youth Sport Experiences

One area of parenting that can be stressful and comes early for many parents is that of youth sport. The majority of children in the United States get exposure to some form of organized sport league (t-ball, flag football, volleyball, etc.) or sport skill development programs (swim, gymnastics) across the preschool and elementary school years, and this arena can bring challenges for many parents, as well as their children. Research has highlighted how parents play a key role in helping their children have positive youth sport experiences.[1] In this chapter, we present strategies parents can use to best equip themselves to be beacons of support and guide their children along the youth sport world in a way that maximizes their experiences and makes the parental experience fun and rewarding.

• **Parents should do their homework in checking out youth sport programs.** One of the most important things parents can do for their children is to check out sport leagues and programs carefully before enrolling their children. Some programs are not set up to provide an appropriate developmental experience for children. There can be many reasons for this. It is possible the people in charge have little knowledge of child and adolescent development, exercise science, and/or principles of education. We find it interesting that sport programs often provide bios of their coaches, and sometimes the only credentials included are their personal sport accomplishments. The fact that coaches played the sport they are coaching is great, but it does not ensure that they have the knowledge to be effective coaches working with young athletes. In fact, young athletes suffer frequently from having coaches who lack knowledge and who have no formal training in coaching, child and adolescent development, pedagogy (methods of coaching/teaching). Often these are the kinds of coaches that do many things (use high levels of punishment, create an ego-involving climate, and vacuum all the fun out of sport). Parents should be confident before enrolling their children that the sport experience is going to be positive, focused on skill building, and provide opportunities for athletes to make friends and be challenged. To make sure this is the case, parents can read available material provided by programs that outlines the mission, speak to sport administrators to ask specific questions about how the program is run, observe the program first-hand when possible, and speak with coaches, athletes, and parents of athletes about their experience in the program to try to get a sense of programs. More specifically, parents can look for or inquire about the following:

❏ Does the program focus on athletic improvement and excellence that can lead to winning or does the emphasis seem to be only on winning?

❏ Does the program emphasize an athlete-centered philosophy that values all participants, considers the needs of athletes, and builds programming that focuses on athlete development?

❏ Is the program known for building positive relationships with athletes, family members, community members?

❏ Does the program emphasize quality coaching from caring coaches, who are trained in the sport?

❏ Are the coaches friendly, positive, and do they care about the athletes?

❏ Do the coaches praise effort and improvement and help all athletes improve?

❏ Does the program emphasize learning skills, learning from mistakes, and navigating adversity to excel in sport and life?

- ❏ Do the athletes look like they are enjoying their participation?
- ❏ Do the athletes improve across the season?
- ❏ Are teammates nice to one another and help one another in practices?
- ❏ Are the athletes respectful to teammates, family, opponents, officials?

- **Parents can promote coaching education in youth sport programs**
  Many youth sport programs are led primarily by volunteer coaches. As a result, sport administrators may feel that the bar should necessarily be set low for coaching credentials since individuals are taking time out of their busy schedules to help out by coaching or taking on other duties to assist the league. While this is logical on the one hand, on the other hand, it is very important to understand the high stakes involved in providing rich and stimulating youth sport opportunities for young athletes. Canada has a system in place that requires youth sport coaches to undergo some basic training before they may coach children. Research has revealed that providing even two hours of training focused on how to create a task-involving climate for young athletes can have a season long impact on children's experiences with the team.[2] Clearly, if parents asked about and were pro-active in encouraging leagues to provide training, more leagues might require basic levels of coaching education. Perhaps it is realistic to think that parents could play an instrumental role in prompting youth sport organizations across the country to require a basic coaching education course for all youth sport coaches in the U.S.

Parents Can Reinforce Each of the Features of a Caring and Task-Involving Climate

Up to this point in the book, our efforts have been directed towards coaches, but in this chapter, we highlight how everything we have discussed so far about creating a caring and task-involving climate can be applied from the parent perspective, and that is where we are headed next, helping parents identify ways they can reinforce the features of this positive and supportive climate. In Climate in Action 11.1, Coach Darren Erpelding describes how he creates (and values having!) a positive relationship with parents. This coach recognizes the important role that parents play in helping athletes have a wonderful sport experience.

CLIMATE IN ACTION 11.1

As a coach of a high school team, parents are a big part of our program. One of the best strategies I've found to be helpful for our team, is to meet with parents at the beginning of the season and share my expectations for them. In this meeting I set boundaries and encourage parents to cheer for and support their athletes as well as the entire team, and to refrain from

CLIMATE IN ACTION 11.1 Continued

coaching (to leave that to me) and to stay off the officials (to also leave that to me). When parents forget this (for example, during a game), I walk over to the stands and ask them to tone it down, and they do. I've noticed that officials really seem to appreciate this. I feel that meeting with parents before the season gives me a chance to convey how much I care about all the kids and want each of them to have a great experience. My parents do a great job helping the team come together and support a family that is experiencing loss (death, illness). They set up meal trains and things like that. I think, overall, parents are a huge asset to our program, and a key to having a great relationship with them is to make sure we are on the same page at the beginning of the season.

Shared by Darren Erpelding

Treating Coaches and Teammates With Mutual Kindness and Respect

•   **Teach athletes gratitude**. One of the best and easiest things parents can do is teach their children to be appreciative of their coaches, and to learn to thank them at the end of every game and practice for their efforts. Even though parents may be paying for the league/lessons/etc., it is still important for children to learn to value the way that others contribute to their growth and development. Parents can encourage their children to listen to, get to know, and allow the coach to get to know them. Parents can foster an appreciation in their children for coaches by making these kinds of comments:

   o   *"Kristina, it's cool that you have coaches who seem like they really enjoy coaching your team."*

   o   *"Linda, your coaches sure are busy people, but they find a way to give your team a lot of practice time; they must really care about you."*

   o   *"Florence, your coaches put a lot of effort into planning practice. I love how it's so organized and how they are thinking what drills to include to help you all the most."*

   o   *"Derek, I could tell your coach was bumming that he sent Chris on that play when he got thrown out at home. Coaches just have to make the best decision they can in the moment, and not worry about it after that."*

   Comments like these highlight for young athletes how they should be appreciative of the efforts of their coaches, and they help the coach reinforce the features of the caring and task-involving climate. It is easy for anyone to let these things go unnoticed, and valuable for young athletes to have parents who help their children make such observations.

- **Officiating is a tougher than it looks**. Parents can also help children understand how difficult it is to be an official. Officials undergo special training and work hard to make the best calls they can. They will make mistakes at times, just like every other human being in the world, but they probably wanted to become an official because they love sport so much, and everyone should always treat them with kindness and respect, even if they make a bad call sometimes. Parents can help children develop emotional regulation on this front. It is easy to get worked up, angry, and frustrated when we perceive an official was not very strong, but in the big picture of life, these experiences are low on the hierarchy of what is important in life. Hospitals are filled with people who are very sick, cities have families that do not have adequate food and shelter, and countries around the world are at war. Dealing with a bad call or the poor performance of an official is challenging, but definitely something that all should be able to deal with in a mature manner, and parents can help their children develop this perspective early on in their sport experience.

- **Help athletes develop empathy for those who struggle with the sport**. Parents can also help their children develop empathy for other young athletes who are slower to develop skills, understand rules and strategies, and who overall progress at a slower speed. Parents can remind their children of areas that are challenging for them (math, keeping their room clean), and highlight for them how some children need a longer period and more practice to achieve at the same level that others reach more quickly. How valuable if children can be taught to recognize and support others who could use extra encouragement. Too often in youth sport, we can observe young athletes who are being very critical of their teammates because they are not throwing strikes, seeing the open teammate, or getting their serve in play.

- **Help athletes develop empathy for those who struggle with social skills**. Parents can also help their children develop empathy to recognize when others on their team may feel socially disconnected, lack confidence, or not be having fun. It is times like these when parents might help their children see the power in reaching out to young athletes and offering to be their partner for a drill, sitting by them on the bleachers before a game, giving them a compliment in some way, or just taking the time to get to know them better. And what would be really huge is parents reminding their athletes to support their teammates, especially in difficult times after they made a mistake or had a poor showing. Michael Robbins expresses this sentiment well in his Ted Talk.[3] Children who learn to be aware and sensitive to what is happening with their teammates are developing an important skill (empathy) that will serve them well outside of sport and across their lives.

Reinforcing Effort and Improvement

- **Parents should make "effort and improvement" their mantra with their children**. If young athletes are asked what their parents care most about in their sport involvement, most parents likely want an answer related to effort and improvement (and fun!!). Parents would want to hear their children say things like, "My parents just want me to give my best effort and have fun; they don't care about winning that much"; "They are not worried that I have to be the best athlete on the team. Really, they want me to make friends, work hard, and have the chance to get better at the sport." Most parents align with this view, but then when it comes time to compete, it is easy for an alter ego to step forward that has a focus on winning and outperforming others. Sure, that is a purpose of sport, but parents are at their best and most helpful when they help children stay focused on things they can control like their high effort, good attitude, and continued improvement.

• **Think before providing comments.** As a follow-up to the last point, it is helpful when parents check their comments before speaking to make sure that everything they say centers around a message that sport is about giving high effort and getting better each day. The stereotype of parental responses is focused on outcome, *"Did you win? Did you get a hit?"* but parents should train themselves early to ask, *"How was the game? Did you have fun? Did you support the coach and your teammates?"*; *"Did you give your best effort from start to finish?"* or as John O'Sullivan, founder of Changing the Game Project suggests, the best thing parents can say is, *"I love watching you play."*[4] Parents would help their children so much by avoiding all talk that results in a negative focus:

o *"Wow, the officials were terrible."*

o *"I can't believe the coach didn't put you in sooner."*

o *"Amy sure had a bad game; I can't understand why the coach gives her so much playing time."*

o *"The other team sure got lucky in the second half."*

These kinds of statements help "stir the pot" of a negative sport experience. It is easy for parents to catch themselves going negative when they do not realize on the front end what an important role they play in helping shape their children's positive sport experiences.

CLIMATE IN ACTION 11.2

Along these lines, it is helpful when parents can draw attention to and help young athletes notice their own effort and improvement in their children, as well as effort and improvement on the part of their coaches, teammates, and opponents. How advantageous when parents can say things like:

- *"Daniel, I love how you kept giving your best effort all throughout the game. It must have been frustrating to watch the opponent get so many hits, but you just stayed determined out there on every play; I'm really proud of you. That is how great athletes play the game."*

CLIMATE IN ACTION 11.2 Continued

- *"Sally, your team was so much better than your opponent today. Your hard work is paying off. It's clear you all are starting to understand how to be in good position, and physically you are in such better shape than at the beginning of the season. Wow, that has to feel good."*
- *"Stan, I thought it was cool that all of you were such good sports. It's hard to lose so badly, and your coaches and teammates treated the other team with kindness and respect. That is how sport is supposed to be played, for sure."*
- *"Akiko, It's crazy how much you have improved your dribble with your nondominant hand. You look so much more comfortable on the court, having that ability to switch hands with the dribble, shoot left handed layups, etc. Can you tell how much you've improved? Isn't that fun to see that improvement in yourself?"*

- Parents should note that many children do not have parents who might be helping them see their own improvement, so it is huge when parents can point out improvement to their children's teammates. Young athletes can benefit from hearing comments like these from their teammates' parents: "*Vicki, your jump shot is looking dope. You've really improved in how high you are getting off the ground, and having that nice follow-through. Good work, girl!*"; or "*Zach, your backhand seems like it's improving every day. I love how you are staying down on the ball and hitting out … impressive, man!*" Parents might also be reminded that young athletes on the opposing team sometimes may not be getting much kudos from parents and coaches, and it is nice when parents can take a nonpartisan approach and compliment their children's opponents.

Mistakes are Part of Learning

Making mistakes is not fun for any of us, and young athletes can feel bad, embarrassed, and discouraged after mistakes. This may be one of the most important areas where parents come into play to help their children learn how to process and deal with life when things are not going their way. So, how can parents help? Here are some thoughts:

- **Help athletes recognize that everyone makes mistakes.** Recently we have watched another round of NFL playoff games where the number of mistakes made was astounding. These professional athletes missed easy field goals, dropped passes that were in their hands, and made errors on running routes. They threw interceptions, failed to see the pass rush, and misread defense alignments. And these are professionals on the best teams in the leagues. They train full-time to play their sport and they have been doing it for years. The fact that they make frequent mistakes should be a reminder to young athletes that mistakes are just part of the game, and the most important thing about making mistakes is how athletes respond after making them. Parents can help children learn that mistakes occur for everyone, and how they respond to mistakes is what it is all about. Responding with a head held high and a commitment to keep working hard is the key, and young athletes should be praised for this reaction. Athletes should be encouraged to embrace that mistakes and development go hand in hand; together they help athletes push themselves, try new things, and expand their skill set.

- **Take care not to over-exaggerate the importance of a sport performance.** Sometimes all involved in sport make sport bigger than it is and bigger than it should be. We notice how professional/college announcers get out of whack speaking about the importance of games. They say things like, *"These athletes are going to think about this game every day the rest of their lives!!!"* in reference to a national championship game. We sure hope not. These athletes are going to live decades longer and we hope they have more important and meaningful experiences in life and know this game is not the be all and end all of their lives. They are going to find soulmates, have children, and engage in meaningful work that makes the world a better place. It is wonderful for individuals to have great sport memories, but how unfortunate when we overplay the importance of a single sporting event. And how crazy when we apply this mentality to youth sport. Parents can be instrumental in helping their children pull the important lessons to be learned from sport, without hyping it as the culmination of their lives to date.

- **Help athletes define mistakes as opportunities to improve.** If individuals never made mistakes and everything always came easy, what a boring life they would have. Strong performances are so much sweeter because of all the mistakes made along the way that give meaning to the best days. Young athletes are not born understanding this concept as a default; they must have it reinforced often by parents, coaches, teachers, and all the significant adults with whom they spend time.

- **Stick to the positive when it comes to providing athletes with feedback.** Sometimes parents fall into the role of dissecting games, and plays, and details of competitions, outlining for young athletes all the ways in which they made mistakes. Parents need to be reminded that the most important role they can play wherever they are (on the sideline, in the car on the way home) is to back off on the analyses and keep the focus on their pride in their children for their effort, even in the midst of mistakes. Parents are much more helpful when they can "catch their children doing good." Parents would love having bosses and supervisors at their worksites who took this approach and supported their effort, encouraged their creativity, and stuck by them when they made mistakes.

Everyone Plays an Important Role

Another feature of a caring and task-involving climate is reinforcing the concept that every single member of the team plays an important role. The team is better because of the contributions of each athlete, and though athletes bring many different attributes to the team, all are vital to the team's overall success. What is interesting on this front is that the contributions of a few athletes are hard to miss. The best athletes and the best performers rarely go unnoticed, and of course their contributions are very important for the team. But in a caring and task-involving climate, everyone understands that these contributions are not more valuable than those of other athletes on the team. Parents play a key role in helping young athletes value the contribution of their teammates, especially in cases where these contributions may be less obvious to all. Here are some examples of how parents can help their athletes value and recognize the innumerable wonderful qualities their teammates bring to the team. Parents could say things like the following:

- *"I love how Zainab gets along with everyone on the team; it really helps having athletes like her because the team is less likely to have little cliques when you have people like Zainab who talk to everyone and become friends with everyone."*
- *"Caleb is so steady out on the court. It's fun to watch him; nothing seems to ruffle his feathers. It seems like he helps the team stay calm."*
- *"Betty is so positive with everyone. I love watching her. Her body language and everything about her makes it look like she is invested and loves being part of the team. etc."*
- *"I like how Max is always talking to the other team in a nice way. It's cool how he is nice and respectful to everyone and yet such an intense competitor at the same time. He makes your team look good."*
- *"I'm really noticing how much Sujean is improving her running form. Her arms look in sync and she's keeping her head up. Her pace has definitely picked up. Do you think she notices how much she has improved?"*
- *"It makes me smile how Kristen isn't the best athlete on the team, but she is the first to arrive at practice and the last to leave. It sure is fun having teammates like her."*

These are a few examples of how parents can be on the lookout to help their athletes recognize some of the sweet qualities that are critical to a team reaching its potential, yet are things that too often go unnoticed. If all parents had it on their radar screens to look and notice these important behaviors and share them with their athletes, it could make a big difference for their children, and for youth sport in general.

Cooperation is Fostered Among Teammates

The last feature of a caring and task-involving climate is helping young athletes foster cooperation among all their teammates. Often teams have great cooperation from a few athletes, or there are little groups of athletes that have this going, but it is special to observe a team where cooperation among all teammates is the standard. Sometimes teams have too much rivalry at the expense of cooperation. Parents can play a large role in helping bring alive this feature, and here are a few tips for thinking about how to make it happen:

• **Parent involvement**. Parents can help schedule a beginning of the season gathering for coaches, athletes, and their families that includes some structured activities designed to help families get to know each other. Without intentionally including some strategies to help athletes and their families get to know each other, these events can sometimes be duds. It is hard to put a finger on why some events do not result in everyone having a good time. It may be that some families are shy and do not find it easy or comfortable to introduce themselves to others. It is possible, too, that it can be intimidating for some athletes and their families if they are new to the team or less connected, and they have the impression that some families are already very tight and connected. Whatever the reason, when planning events (cook out; pizza party), it is a great idea to include ice breakers or activities that might help families get to know each other in a fun and not too over-the-top way. Here are some suggestions:

  o **Have everyone wear name tags**. It is hard to remember names and this helps individuals reinforce names and connect athletes with their families. Have everyone put a first name in large print so everyone can see the writing.

  o **Pair up athletes and have them bring their families together to meet**. Let each child introduce his/her family to the teammate's family. This is a great exercise for children to be given the responsibility of making introductions. There could be several rotations of this activity whereby every athlete introduces his/her family to the families of three to four teammates. Probably 5–7 minutes could be used for each rotation.

  o **Try speed "friendship."** A team version of speed dating could also be used where the group splits up into two equal groups, with each forming a circle. One of the circles is on the inside facing outward, and the second group is on the outside facing inward. This leaves every individual facing a partner. The leader could call out a question, "What is your favorite sport movie and why?" and allow a minute for the pairs to discuss the questions with each other. After a minute (or whatever amount of time is needed) the individuals on the inside of the circle rotate, and everyone has a new partner. The leader asks the next question,

    • *"What is your favorite moment watching or playing volleyball and why?"*;
      "Who is your favorite athlete and why?";
    • *"Which game of the season are you most looking forward to this season?"*;

- *"What do you like to do to relax after a stressful day?"*; or
- *"Tell your partner about your pets."*

    These questions are light and help individuals get to know each other. They open the door for future conversations, and they are fun.

o   **Family outings.** Tina Syer, of the Positive Coaching Alliance, likes to have youth sport family outings where the families play in a scrimmage game with or against the athletes.[5] How fun for parents to get a chance to interact with the athletes on the team in a lighthearted activity early in the season that is great for all involved. A plus is that athletes see right away how much fun it is to cooperate with one another in a positive climate.

    The point of these activities is that thought is given ahead of time of fun ways to foster interaction among athletes and their families. It is fun to be creative and come up with new ideas. The internet is filled with clever ideas to adapt for such purposes.

- **Talk about what cooperation with teammates looks like.** Parents can have discussions with their athletes about what cooperation with all teammates might look like. Often, athletes describe their experiences on teams where there was definitely not cooperation among all teammates (athletes cheered for only some teammates; athletes invited some of the team to the lake house/a birthday party; athletes wanted some teammates to do poorly so their friends would get more playing time), so athletes may have great insight on what cooperation looks like and what might help or hinder it. Encouraging athletes to think hard about how they can bond and support each member of their team is a great place to start.

- **Talk about what leadership looks like with athletes.** We observe at times that one of the barriers to fostering cooperation, is athletes' misunderstanding of leadership and seniority. Sometimes athletes who are the oldest believe that they deserve special treatment, and engage in behaviors that are antithetical (call out athletes when their own behavior is lacking; go through the food line first and hoard) to cooperation among all, such as teasing and putting down others on the team, leaving teammates out of conversations, forming subgroups that are exclusive, and being insensitive to words that are spoken. Real leaders know how to build up others, lead by example, and be inclusive of all. All athletes can be leaders in terms of building a sense of cooperation with each of their teammates.

Last Tips for Sport Parents

- **Get to know all athletes and their parents.** Parents become difference makers when they make an effort to get to know all parents and every athlete on the team. The African saying, "It takes a village to raise a child" is right on the mark, and is true for youth sport: "It takes a village to help every young athlete have a great sport experience." Coaches cannot create a caring and task-involving climate alone. Parents play an incredible role when they step forward and look for all the ways that they can bring the climate to life.

- **Share the caring and task-involving climate philosophy with all who know their children.** Parents should never assume that others have been exposed to and bought in to this approach, so they should share the philosophy with all who interact with their children. For example, if grandparents visit and reinforce the importance of winning, being the best, and extrinsic factors, it runs counter to the message parents are sending and is not helpful.

- **Allow athletes to face challenges.** It is very difficult to allow children to struggle, to be disappointed, and to experience failure, and often parents are doing all they can to help their children avoid these experiences. However, as hard as it is, parents need to allow their children room to make mistakes and deal with them, to be disappointed, and to know that part of life is learning to handle things that do not always go the way they want them to. Good parents recognize this fundamental aspect and help their children see the upside of downsides, that mistakes are great vehicles for learning and provide wonderful opportunities to learn and grow. What makes this possible is athletes knowing they can return to home base where mom, dad (parents, guardians) are there to love and support them no matter what.

- **Protect all athletes from coaching abuse.** Parents should never forget their role in protecting their children. Sometimes parents are slow to realize that coaches have crossed the line into abusive behavior, but parents should not allow their children to ever be verbally, emotionally, or physically abused. Athletes should be removed immediately from such environments and this kind of coaching behavior should be reported.

- **Youth sport should not be focused on developing professional athletes.** Parents should frequently remind themselves that something like one-half of 1 percent of youth athletes ever go on to play professional sport. Clearly, we should not be setting up the youth sport world for the purpose of developing professional athletes. Instead, what if we created an environment where kids can, as the Positive Coaching Alliance, suggests, become "Better Athletes, Better People" through their participation in youth sport. Children learning to move skillfully during their childhood years sets the stage for them to enjoy and feel comfortable being physically active across their entire lives.

*****

If parents engaged in the behaviors described in this chapter on a large scale, the potential would be there to totally change the world of youth sport. All young athletes would be in a position to have positive sport experiences, learning lessons that they carry with them through life.

Reflecting on My Sport Parenting Behavior

It's helpful for parents to stop and reflect on the concepts present in this chapter and to think about what they are doing well, and the avenues for improvement.

- What is my perception of how I support my child in sport?
- What would I speculate is my child's perception of the degree to which I support him/her in sport?
- How am I doing on these fronts?:
  o Encouraging my child to treat coaches and teammates with kindness and respect
  o Helping my child recognize and value effort and improvement
  o Reinforcing that mistakes are part of learning
  o Helping foster cooperation among my child's teammates
  o Assisting my child in seeing that everyone plays an important role on the team.
- What strategies could I try that are suggested in this chapter or that I'm thinking of that could help me highlight these features with my child?
  o Encouraging my child to treat coaches and teammates with kindness and respect.
  o Helping my child recognize and value effort and improvement
  o Reinforcing that mistakes are part of learning
  o Helping foster cooperation among my child's teammates
  o Assisting my child in seeing that everyone plays an important role on the team.

Sources

[1]   Thompson, J. (2008). *Positive sport parenting: How "second-goal" parents raise winners in life through sports*. Balance Sports.

[2]   Smith, R. & Smoll, F. (2012). *Sport psychology for youth sport coaches*. Lanham, MD: Rowman & Littlefield.

[3]   Robbins, M. (2014). Change the game of youth sport. Retrieved April 21, 2019: https://mike-robbins.com/tedx/

[4]   O'Sullivan, J. (2019). Changing the Game Project: John O'Sullivan. Retrieved April 21, 2019: https://changingthegameproject.com/

[5]   Syer, T. (2019). Establishing positive culture on youth sport teams. Retrieved April 21, 2019: Positive coaching alliance video, Tina Syer: www.youtube.com/watch?v=MDNXZ5-rVS8

12

THE ROLE OF ADMINISTRATORS IN CREATING A CARING AND TASK-INVOLVING CLIMATE

Highlights

- Administrators can seek to align the organizational mission with a caring and task-involving climate.
- Administrators can create sport programming that aligns with climate.
- Providing coach education training related to climate reinforces the importance a developing positive approach to coaching.
- Administrators can model features of a caring and task-involving climate.
- Assessment practices can be aligned with features of a caring and task-involving climate.

Other key people needed to create and sustain a caring and task-involving climate are sport program administrators. As leaders of the organization, they set the vision for the organization and influence the organizational climate, both of which can make it easier or harder for coaches to nurture a caring and task-involving climate. Therefore, administrators should also reflect upon their role in creating a caring and task-involving climate. This chapter reviews some concrete considerations for administrators.

Align Organizational Mission with a Caring and Task-involving Climate

> *Outstanding people have one thing in common: An absolute sense of mission.*
>
> *Zig Ziglar[1]*

A mission is key to any organization as it highlights what values are important within the organization and helps define appropriate behaviors within the organization. Therefore, the first way administrators can support coaches in the development of a caring and task-involving climate is to ensure that the organization's mission aligns with the features of the climate. Administrators may want to look at their mission and ask the following questions:

❏ Does the mission focus on athletic improvement and excellence that can lead to winning or does our mission focus only on winning?

❏ Does the mission emphasize an athlete-centered philosophy that values all participants, considers the needs of athletes, and builds programming that focuses on athlete development?

❏ Does the mission focus on building relationships with athletes, family members, community members?

❏ Does the mission emphasize quality coaching from caring coaches, who are trained in the sport, practice planning and execution, and safe physical and emotional sporting practices?

❏ Does the mission emphasize the importance of building personal and social responsibility skills (that is, effort, accountability, ownership, teamwork, cooperation, supportiveness)?

❏ Does the mission emphasize learning skills, learning from mistakes, and navigating adversity to excel in sport and life?

A sample mission statement that incorporates these elements might look like this:

> *At ABC Aquatics, we focus on athletes' physical, emotional, and social development through quality coaching conducted in a positive and respectful environment. We pride ourselves on developing positive relationships with swimmers and their families and emphasize achieving personal excellence in and out of the pool.*

An example of an actual program with a mission aligned with a caring and task-involving climate is the Soccer Organization of the Charlottesville Area.[2] Their mission reads:

> *The Soccer Organization of the Charlottesville Area (SOCA) provides all youth and adults superior, comprehensive soccer programming emphasizing player development, enjoyment and citizenship. SOCA is dedicated to serving the local, regional, and national soccer communities.*

This mission has a connection to athlete development (improvement, athlete-centered, learning skills), enjoyment (focused on creating a positive and fun environment), and citizenship (developing life skills and responsibility and a sense of community). This mission is reinforced by the core values also noted on their website.[2]

Another important administrative consideration related to the mission is whether the mission is aligned with the needs of the customers, in this case athletes and their families. Organizations often conduct needs assessments to determine organizational initiatives and programming. For youth sport organizations, this needs assessment can relate to the type of climate athletes would prefer. Interestingly, some research exists that has explored why young athletes participate or drop out of sport and what they consider enjoyable about sport. One of these research studies is worth mentioning. Amanda Visek and her colleagues asked young soccer athletes to identify what made soccer fun.[3] The researchers developed FUN Integration Maps that outlined 11 fun factors. The athletes indicated that soccer was fun when they were trying hard in practice and games, learning and improving in the sport, playing for respectful and friendly coaches, having supportive teammates and developing friendships with them, having a positive game experience (that is, getting a chance to play and demonstrate their skills in front of a supportive audience in a game that is fairly refereed and appropriately challenging), having quality practice sessions, and having team rituals and swag. It is clear from this research that features of a caring and task-involving climate correspond to the fun factors, further suggesting the need to focus on these features to encourage greater enjoyment, which can make it more likely that athletes will continue with the program.

Once a mission is developed, program administrators should share it with all stakeholders in the organization including administrative staff, coaches, parents, athletes, and community to ensure that everyone knows and can begin to live the mission. Administrators might also consider sharing the mission with other organizations in their league or conference and encourage the adoption of a league-wide mission that embraces features of a caring and task-involving climate.

Create Sport Opportunities that Support Features of a Caring and Task-involving Climate

> Don't wait for opportunity. Create it.
>
> *Sue Baker*[4]

In order for youth athletes to demonstrate effort and improvement, they must be provided time to practice and opportunities to play. These opportunities not only allow them to develop their motor memory, but also see how their efforts during play pays off with greater improvement enhancing their confidence for playing sport. Further, great amounts of practice and opportunities to play provide coaches more chances to give instructional feedback to foster improvement, help athletes learn from their mistakes and correct their errors, and encourage and reward effort. Unfortunately, many youth sport programs for young children (ages 6 to 12) do not have many practice opportunities. Rather, the focus is on competitive events emphasizing that only competing and winning matters, whether program administrators intend to send this message or not. Therefore, program administrators need to think strategically about how they can create opportunities that reinforce a task-involving climate through their sport programming. Here are a few ideas:

- **Develop youth sport schedules that encourage learning and improving.** This would include a move from competitive event scheduling to practice scheduling. For example, a program can have practice two or three times a week during a season with few competitive events throughout the season. Practices would emphasize development of fundamental movement skills[5] and basic sport skills along with small-sided games or scrimmages.
- **Encourage athletes to play different sports and different positions within the same sport to improve their overall physical and psychological development.** Athletes who have a better understanding of all positions on the court or field will become better team players and understand their teammates who play these positions. Additionally, athletes who play multiple sports can have fewer injuries, more motivation and enjoyment, and be a more well-rounded athlete.[6] Therefore, programs can help athletes improve their development by instituting rules that promote diversification. For example, create a program rule where players need to rotate positions throughout the athletic season. Additionally, administrators could develop a program that avoids early specialization by not offering year-round sport participation in a single sport but rather develop yearly participation where young athletes play a different sport every season with the same coach who is trained as a multiple sport coach.
- **Encourage parents to engage in deliberate play.**[7] Administrators can provide parents basic sport skills training and then provide weekly idea sheets that incorporate the skills into fun play that parents can initiate outside of practice sessions throughout the season. This use of deliberate play will encourage parents to be active with their young athletes, emphasize the importance of practice in improving sport skills, and remind everyone that developing sport skills can be fun and can be played throughout life.
- **Involve more individuals in middle and high school sport programming.** Within middle and high school sport programming, administrators can consider ways for more individuals to be involved in sport skill development. Athletic and activity administrators can think creatively about how coaches may be able to contribute to comprehensive school physical activity programs[8] through intramural and extramural programming before and/or after school. This can even be extended to other members of the family, like brothers and sisters, to practice building relationships.

Provide Coach Education Training for Coaches

It's what you learn after you know it all that counts.

John Wooden[9]

Training sport coaches on how to implement a caring and task-involving climate is another valuable strategy for administrators to consider. This training would entail a two-pronged approach. The first prong would focus on training in fundamental skills and sport technique and tactics, training in organizing effective practices with appropriate drills, and training on how to coach sports (for example, demonstrate skills, provide appropriate challenges, understand developmentally appropriate practice). This type of training sets the stage for youth to learn and improve, apply effort in meaningful ways, and feel appropriately supported in their endeavors to excel. For example, youth sport program administrators might consider the following:

- Become a member organization with the National Alliance for Youth Sports (www.nays.org/), which provides training for administrators, coaches, and parents along with additional resources for youth sport programming.
- Use online resources such as iCoachKids (www.icoachkids.eu/), which offers free online resources and training for youth sport coaches.
- Reach out to a local college or university to see about a collaboration with a teacher/scholar who would be willing to provide youth sport training.

The second prong would focus on training coaches to create a caring and task-involving climate. The strategies offered in this book would be a good starting point for this training. Additionally, youth sport program administrators could reach out to coach education programs that focus on developing a caring and task-involving climate. One exemplar program is the Positive Coaching Alliance, an organization that focuses on helping coaches create a positive sport experience for youth (www.positivecoach.org/). They offer several training programs as well as free online resources to help administrators, coaches, and parents develop a positive coaching environment by emphasizing many of the features of the caring and task-involving climate. Following training, coaches should also be able to see the climate in action, develop strategies aligned with their own personality and philosophy, implement new strategies with feedback from observers, and discuss successes and struggles with building the climate with other coaches. Therefore, fostering coach development becomes a critical role for program administrators. This two-pronged approach to training would certainly set the stage for coaches to successfully implement a caring and task-involving climate.

Model a Caring and Task-involving Climate with Coaches

Leadership is the capacity to translate vision into reality.

Warren Bennis[10]

Another effective way to promote a caring and task-involving climate, is for administrators to model the features of the climate to their coaches so they can see it in action. While the strategies articulated in this book have focused on how coaches can apply the features of the climate in their sport environment, these strategies can easily be adapted by program administrators to use with their coaches. Here are just a few modeling examples:

- Administrators can hire coaches that align with the organizational mission and have a commitment to an athlete-centered philosophy. By doing so, program administrators model that a holistic coaching philosophy is important and that it will be a priority within the organization.
- Administrators can be accessible and get to know all of the coaches and identify their needs and ways that administrators can support their sport program and help them develop as a coach.
- Administrators can model empathy, self-control, and understanding toward community members and program participants.
- Administrators can observe coaches in practice and give feedback aligned with a task-involving climate. The focus should be on helping them develop and improve as a coach. Additionally, administrators can help coaches learn from their own mistakes in a supportive way. These observations and learnings can be combined with a peer mentoring programming. Once coaches have developed a sense of the climate and have been through an observation with an administrator, they can be assigned to mentor other coaches within the program.
- Administrators can approach all disciplinary situations with empathy and understanding.
- Administrators can support coaches by giving them appropriate resources and compensation to allow them to do their job effectively.
- Administrators can establish a sense of community among all coaches by making them feel they are a valued member of the program, giving them a voice in the direction of the organization, and encouraging them to support one another.
- Administrators can show collaboration by creating a community advisory board that can provide resources and expertise to help the program thrive. For example, a community advisory board may be made up of coaches, parents, college/university faculty, and local community leaders who work together to provide resources for the program, consider ways to evaluate and improve the program, and promote its good work.

Modeling practices we want to see coaches exhibit with their athletes will not only help coaches learn ways to implement these features in their own practice but also recognize that this is important to the organizational mission.

Develop Assessment Practices that Support a Caring and Task-involving Climate

The greatest of faults, I should say, is to be conscious of none.

Thomas Carlyle[11]

Coach Assessment Practices

Helping coaches improve through comprehensive assessment practices is essential for their professional development and ensures that coach practices are aligned with the organizational mission. Several excellent resources exist for coach assessments[12, 13] and many administrators already assess coaches and hold them accountable for quality coaching practice. However, program administrators will want to consider whether current evaluation practices assess how well coaches are implementing a caring and task-involving climate. Here are some assessment criteria for program administrators to consider:

- Coach develops positive relationships with the team (individual athletes and team).
- Coach creates a team environment based on mutual respect.
- Coach creates a physically safe sport environment.
- Coach creates an emotionally safe sport environment.
- Coach does not bully, berate, or demean athletes.
- Coach demonstrates effective practice planning that assists in skill development and allows for sufficient time for improvement.
- Coach provides effective instructional feedback.
- Coach recognizes effort and improvement.
- Coach encourages athletes to learn from mistakes.
- Coach works with every athlete to help him/her improve.
- Coach reinforces for each athlete her/his value to the team.
- Coach encourages athletes to work with and support other members of the team.
- Athletes demonstrate improvements in sport skills.
- Athletes demonstrate improvements in life skills.
- Athletes report improvements in their sport skills and increased confidence.
- Athletes report liking the coach and team and feeling supported by the coach.
- Athletes exhibit kindness toward others.
- Athletes do not engage in bullying or hazing practices.
- Athletes report a positive and enjoyable sport experience.

By conducting an assessment with coaches, program administrators are given the opportunity to praise coaches for what is going well and seek to offer advice and assistance in helping them develop into better coaches.

Another consideration in assessment practices is educating parents and fans on coach effectiveness. Some family members and fans may consider winning percentage and team titles to be the only indicators of coaching effectiveness. Therefore, it will be imperative to share with the public the program mission, what matters within this sport program, and how coaches are assessed in line with these values. However, a program administrator may also want to address the misconception that winning equals excellent coaching. Here are some arguments to consider:

- A winning season may certainly say something about coach effectiveness but it also might be the luck of the draw that a coach has a team of naturally talented athletes or athletes that are early maturers.
- Developing a winning tradition takes time as athletes develop skills and tactics. We see this discussed often in high school and collegiate sport as commentators note a coach losing a lot of seniors and is embarking on a building year.
- A coach with a winning season may be relieved of duties because the coach manipulated the system by using practices that were not always fair or within the spirit of the game or the coach achieved a winning season at the expense of teaching life lessons.

Program Assessment Practices

Program administrators may also be interested in assessing the overall effectiveness of their programs. Using the program mission, administrators develop goals to assess effectiveness. One goal could relate to evaluating the effectiveness of implementing and supporting a caring and task-involving climate. While coach assessments are part of program assessment practices, it is important to recognize that other key stakeholders within the organization as well as social and cultural practices within the community or sport world that may need to improve to foster a caring and task-involving climate. Program assessments can be extensive or brief and formal or informal (see the Reflecting on Practice section for an example of a brief informal assessment tool). The key to a good program assessment is that it provides useful information that can help a program improve its practice. For example, the Women's Intersport Network (WIN) for KC, in collaboration with the University of Kansas developed a small and informal survey that was very helpful for their program (see Climate in Action 12.1).[14]

CLIMATE IN ACTION 12.1

WIN for KC hosts a summer sports camp for girls based around the features of the caring and task-involving climate. The University of Kansas Sport and Exercise Psychology (KUSEP) Lab worked with the program coordinators to help them improve their program. They began by observing the summer sport camp and talking with the program coordinator. They then developed a short survey for athletes to complete following the camp. This survey had items that assessed the girls' perceptions of the climate, their enjoyment level, and whether they liked the leaders and other campers. The results were

---

CLIMATE IN ACTION 12.1 Continued

shared with the program coordinator and suggestions for improvement were made. Members of the KUSEP Lab worked with the program coordinator and staff to institute training for their camp counselors that further helped them improve the caring and task-involving climate. The camp was already doing a great job providing a wonderful camp experience for girls, and the partnership with a local university helped the short-handed sport program obtain expertise to gather feedback from the young athletes, their parents, and the volunteer camp counselors. The camp administrator received a report that could be shared with parents and on the website to show how they are doing all they can to create the best camp experience possible.[14]

As program assessments can be very time-consuming work, program administrators can develop a community advisory board to help conduct the program assessment. By utilizing experts in assessment design, coach education, and sport psychology from the local college/university and gathering insights from coaches, staff, and parents, program administrators can develop a team that provides a strong program assessment along with practical suggestions for program improvements.

*****

Program administrators play a key role in the success and sustainability of sport organizations including the climate created. It really comes down to leadership. If administrators develop the organizational mission, model the mission, create sport opportunities that support the mission and align coach training and evaluation practices with a caring and task-involving climate, it will be more likely to occur.

Reflecting on Practice

Consider the ideas presented in this chapter and reflect on how you might incorporate them to improve your organization. Here are two exercises to consider.

Develop a Mission Statement and Live By It

If your organization does not have a vision statement and a mission statement, create them. Here is a link to a resource that will help in creating a mission statement: https://topnonprofits.com/wp-content/uploads/2012/09/Mission-Vision-Worksheet.pdf. Remember to consider how the caring and task-involving climate might be represented in the statements.

Once developed, consider three to five actions that you can take in the next year to realize your vision. These actions might also apply to others in your organization, such as the coaches and staff. If not, create three to five actions that they can take that will support the mission. Remember to consider how you will evaluate whether you and your staff have accomplished the actions and move the organization closer to achieving its mission.

Gather Feedback to Assist in Program Improvement

Find out what your athletes are thinking and feeling about the climate created in your sport program and how it connects to their own behavior. Here are some potential questions to help you get a sense of how things are going and where you can improve. Following each question is the chapter that describes more about the feature of the climate or the benefits of the climate. These questions could even be adjusted for family members to complete.

Directions: Think about your experiences on your sport team this season. Circle whether you agree (thumbs up), neutral (sideways finger) or disagree (thumbs down) with each statement.

1. My coach supported me this season. (Ch. 3)	👍	👉	👎
2. Our team is respectful and kind to one another. (Ch. 3)	👍	👉	👎
3. I got to know many of the athletes on the team. (Ch. 3)	👍	👉	👎
4. I get recognized and praised for my effort and improvement. (Ch. 4)	👍	👉	👎
5. I was encouraged to learn from my mistakes. (Ch. 5)	👍	👉	👎
6. I really felt like part of the team. (Ch. 6)	👍	👉	👎
7. I had an important role on the team. (Ch. 6)	👍	👉	👎
8. I was encouraged to help others on the team learn their skills. (Ch. 7)	👍	👉	👎

9. Our team works well together. (Ch. 7)	👍	☞	👎
10. I worked really hard this season. (Ch. 2)	👍	☞	👎
11. I improved my skills this season. (Ch. 2)	👍	☞	👎
12. I enjoyed playing on this team. (Ch. 2)	👍	☞	👎
13. I feel more confident in playing this sport. (Ch. 2)	👍	☞	👎
14. I want to play on this team next year. (Ch. 2)	👍	☞	👎

How to Score the Survey: Use the following instructions to score the survey:

1. Assign a number to each item. A thumbs up (👍) gets a 3, a sideways finger (☞) gets a 2, and a thumbs down (👎) gets a 1.
2. Add up items 1–9. This total score represents the overall climate created on the team. This will range from 9 to 27 with the higher the score meaning the more positive the climate the coach created from the athletes' perspective. Add up all the surveys completed by program participants to get an average score (this can be done for the whole program or by team).
3. Add up items 10–14. This overall score provides information regarding the positive benefits gained from participating in the program. This will range from 5 to 15 with the higher the score meaning the better the benefits were for the athlete. Add up all the surveys completed by program participants to get an average score (this can be done for the whole program or by team).

How to Use the Survey Findings: There are many ways that administrators can use the survey findings. Here are a few suggestions.

1. Administrators can use this survey to determine how well they and the program coaches are creating a caring and task-involving climate. If scores are below 18, it means that more work is needed to make sure structures are in place to support a caring and task-involving climate. This could mean updating and enacting a mission aligned with the climate and/or helping coaches implement features of a caring and task-involving climate through coach education and coach development. Administrators can even tabulate the survey items by feature (for example, just add item 1, 2, and 3 to look at mutual kindness and respect) to see how the program is doing relative to each feature.
2. Administrators can share the survey findings with the community to show how the program is fostering a positive climate and benefiting the athletes.
3. If administrators are familiar with statistics, they could look at the correlation between the overall features of the climate and the positive benefits to show community members that when the features of the climate increase so do the benefits to athletes.

Sources

1. Walters, L. (2000). *Secrets of superstar speakers: Wisdom from the greatest motivators of our time and with those these superstars inspired to dramatic and lasting change.* New York, NY: McGraw Hill, [p. 96].

2. Strategic Plan (2019). Retrieved from www.socaspot.org/about/strategic-plan/

3. Visek, A. J., Achrati, S. M., Manning, H., McDonnell, K. Harris, B. S., & DiPietro, L. (2015). The fun integration theory: Towards sustaining children and adolescents sport participation. *Journal of Physical Activity & Health, 12,* 424–433. Retrieved from www.ncbi.nlm.nih.gov/pmc/articles/PMC4201634/

4. Baker, S. (2016). *Don't wait for opportunity create it!* Create Space Independent Publishing Platform.

5. Fundamental Movement Skills. (n.d.). Retrieved from https://goodhabitsforlife.act.gov.au/kids-at-play/fundamental-movement-skills-fms-1

6. Jayanthi, N., Pinkham, C., Dugas, L., Patrick, B., & LaBella, C. (2013). Sports specialization in young athletes: Evidence-based recommendations. *Sports Health, 5*(3), 251–257. Retrieved from www.ncbi.nlm.nih.gov/pmc/articles/PMC3658407/?_escaped_fragment_=po=0.909091

7. Foundation 1, 2, 3. (n.d.). Retrieved from www.clearinghouseforsport.gov.au/knowledge_base/high_performance_sport/athlete_pathways_and_development/Athlete_Pathways_and_Development/foundation#Foundation2

8. CDC (2015, September 25). *Comprehensive school physical activity program (CSPAP).* Retrieved from www.cdc.gov/healthyschools/physicalactivity/cspap.htm

9. Williams, P. & Denney, J. (2011). *Coach Wooden: The 7 principles that shaped his life and will change yours.* Grand Rapids, MI: Revell, [p. 107].

10. Booher, D. (1991). *Executive's portfolio of model speeches for all occasions.* Englewood Cliffs, NJ: Prentice Hall, [p. 34].

11. Carlyle, T. (1840). On heroes, hero-worship, and the heroic in history. Retrieved from www.gutenberg.org/files/1091/1091-h/1091-h.htm

12. Mercier, R. & Werthner, P. (2007). *Handbook on performance review of coaches.* Coaching Association of Canada. Retrieved from www.saskcoach.ca/pdf/performanceReview.pdf

13. Knutson, C. (February, 2018). 3 ways to evaluate your youth sport coaches. Retrieved from www.myteamgenius.com/blog/3-ways-to-evaluate-your-youth-sport-coaches/

14. Glover, K. & Fry, M. D. (2018). Helping WIN for KC provide a winning environment for girls in their summer sport camps. *Journal of Sport Psychology in Action.* Retrieved from https://doi.org/10.1080/21520704.2018.1509163

PART IV
Conclusion

13

BRINGING IT ALL TOGETHER

Highlights

- Coaches can use the PACE model to slowly and intentionally implement features of the caring and task-involving climate.
- Coaches can share the features of the caring and task-involving climate with others.

In interviewing athletes of a successful female coach, one of her former players stated the following:

> Her innate decency spilled out and soaked every player. Her game successes on the field and the court were record breaking and legendary, but more important, were the hundreds (that number may be low) of young people she influenced beyond game results. I doubt anyone left a team she coached not being a better human being.[1]

This summarizes what many coaches hope to accomplish in their coaching, that is, helping their athletes develop as people. Throughout this book, we have identified the type of climate and associated strategies that can help to set the stage for this development. By engaging in and encouraging mutual respect and kindness (Chapter 3), valuing and reinforcing effort and improvement (Chapter 4), treating mistakes as part of learning (Chapter 5), recognizing the important contribution of all team members (Chapter 6), and fostering a cooperative environment (Chapter 7), coaches create a caring and task-involving climate for all members of their sport team like their coaching staff, team members, athletes' family members, and administrators. A sport team underpinned by a caring and task-involving climate then becomes a place where everyone has an opportunity to belong and feel appreciated by others, a place where everyone has an opportunity to grow and reach their potential as

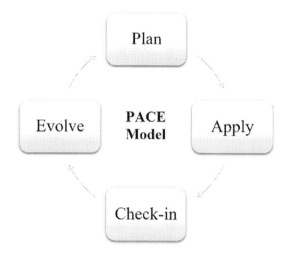

FIGURE 13.1 The PACE Model

an athlete and as a person, and a place where there are opportunities for everyone (coaches, team members, parents, administrators) to contribute in meaningful ways. Our applied and scholarly work, as described in the examples provided in this book, have demonstrated to us the power of creating such a climate and the benefits it can have for young athletes and coaches. In the end, we hope that those exposed to caring and task-involving climates will go out and create this type of environment in their own communities. In so doing, we keep the movement going to create positive youth sport experiences that help others to flourish.

So what is the next step? We encourage coaches to continue their journey of developing a quality youth sport experience by considering how they will implement a caring and task-involving climate in an intentional way on their sport team as systematically suggested in Chapter 8. We recognize that coaching is a developmental process in which one strives to get better over time. Therefore, we offer the PACE model for coaches to use to slowly pace and intentionally implement the climate in their own coaching practice (see Figure 13.1). The PACE model includes four key steps: plan, apply, check-in, and evolve and is based on the cyclical process for improvement in coach practice from the International Sport Coaching Framework.[2]

PACE Model for Developing a Caring and Task-involving Climate

Plan

Coaches can begin by planning what strategies they would like to implement during their season. In choosing strategies we recommend coaches begin by choosing one to three strategies from each feature of the caring and task-involving climate (see Chapters 3–7). One of the benefits of the book is that it provides many strategies and experiences from which to choose. However, we encourage coaches not to see this book as a set of strategies that can be pulled out and readily applied to their setting but as an opportunity for reflection and planning. We recommend that coaches consider strategies that resonate for them as this will ensure the strategies authentically align with their personality, coaching style, and coaching philosophy. Further, we suggest coaches reflect upon their coaching context and athletes coached as this will have implications for which strategies may be most useful. Finally, we remind coaches that creating a caring and task-involving climate is the end result rather than a means to an end. That is, caring coaches do not care for athletes to get them to engage in particular behavior or activities; they care because they are genuinely concerned about each athlete's development and well-being.

Once coaches have identified some strategies, we encourage coaches to plan how these strategies can be implemented during key points of the season like during tryouts, when the season begins, during competitions, and at the end of the season as well as in the day to day practice sessions (see Chapter 8 for examples).

Apply

With a plan in place, coaches can integrate the strategies into their coaching practice. We encourage coaches to begin by considering how they will apply strategies during planned periods throughout the season. Additionally, we recommend coaches develop a system for reminding themselves about their day to day strategies. Coaches can put a key message on their clipboard (for example, emphasize improvement, listen first, make a connection), upload a picture on their smartphone home screen that represents their daily intention (for example, a photo of a coach giving a high five to an athlete as a reminder to recognize and praise each person, a photo of a coach providing individual instruction as a reminder to help each athlete improve), or place it into their daily calendar in order to receive a daily push notification before practice (for example, recognize five athletes on their effort or caring behaviors today in practice, or following competition day's structure practice to help athletes learn from mistakes).

Check-in

Periodically, coaches can check-in to see how they are doing in their development of the caring and task-involving climate. This evaluation can be a personal self-reflection (see reflective activity in Chapter 2) or by engaging in conversations with athletes and their family members to determine their impression of the climate and the season. Coaches can also ask other coaches or administrators to observe their practices to determine how well they are doing at implementing their climate strategies in practice.

Evolve

The last step of the model is for coaches to use information gathered from their check-ins to continue to learn, grow, and evolve. If the application of the strategies is going well then coaches can embrace their success in a job well done. Coaches then might reflect on additional ways they can integrate a caring and task-involving climate into their coach practice. That is, continue to engage in the slow and intentional process of developing as a coach using the PACE model.

As no one is perfect, coaches may also find that some strategies are just not working well. If this is the case, coaches can learn from their mistakes. They can make adjustments in how they apply strategies or choose to engage in different strategies, that is, revisit the planning process.

Share the Climate with Others

An intentional plan for creating a caring and task-involving climate not only involves coaches working to apply effective strategies in their coaching practice, but also getting parents and administrators on board. We encourage coaches to share Chapters 11 and 12 with parents and administrators so they can help promote a caring and task-involving climate. We would also remind coaches to apply the features of the caring and task-involving climate, that is, acting with kindness and respect toward others, encouraging cooperative behavior, and helping members learn from mistakes, when working with parents and administrators.

*****

Our work in this area has helped us to identify many strategies that can be used to create a caring and task-involving climate and we are happy to share them. However, we recognize that each coach and program is unique. Therefore, we encourage coaches to think critically and creatively to determine how to implement the features of the climate in their own practice and adjust the strategies we provided to fit their own coaching style and context. As we know, there is an art and science to coaching. We hope coaches find this book helpful and we wish them the best as they continue their journey in creating a caring and task-involving climate. Thank you for making the effort to become a better coach and to provide even better sport experiences for your athletes.

Learn More

Within this book, we have tried to provide resources and strategies to help coaches learn about and apply features of a caring and task-involving climate. However, we recognize that coaches may want to learn more about the caring and task-involving climate and additional ways to implement it. Here are some resources we would recommend:

- Cronin, C. & Armour, K. (2018). *Care in sport coaching: Pedagogical cases.* London, UK: Routledge.
- Hellison, D. (2011). *Teaching personal and social responsibility through physical activity* (3rd ed.). Champaign, IL: Human Kinetics.
- Orlick, T. (2015). *In pursuit of excellence: How to win in sport and life through mental training.* Champaign, IL: Human Kinetics.
- Shields, D. L. & Bredemeier, B. L. (2009). *True competition: A guide to pursuing excellence in sport and society.* Champaign, IL: Human Kinetics.
- Smoll, F. & Smith, R. (2002). *Way to go, coach!* Portola Valley, CA: Warde Publishers.
- Thompson, J. (2008). *Positive sport parenting.* Portola Valley, CA: Balance Sports Publishing.
- Thompson, J. (2013). *Developing better athletes, better people: A leader's guide to transforming high school and youth sports.* Portola, CA: Balance Sports Publishing.

Reflecting on Practice

Using the PACE Model

Your journey toward improving your engagement in a caring and task-involving climate begins by using the PACE model. Below is a framework that you might find helpful.

Plan

Referring back to Chapters 3 through 7, consider the strategies 1, 2, or 3 below that you could implement, which align with your philosophy, coaching style, coaching context, and athletes.

Engage in and encourage mutual respect and kindness

Strategy 1 _____

Strategy 2 _____

Strategy 3 _____

Value and reinforce effort and improvement

Strategy 1 _____

Strategy 2 _____

Strategy 3 _____

Treat mistakes as part of learning

Strategy 1 _____

Strategy 2 _____

Strategy 3 _____

Recognize the important contribution of all team members

Strategy 1 _____

Strategy 2 _____

Strategy 3 _____

Fostering a cooperative environment

Strategy 1 _____

Strategy 2 _____

Strategy 3 _____

Apply

Identify when you might use these strategies in coaching practice and reminders that you might set for yourself throughout the season.

Pre-season Strategies

_____

_____

_____

_____

Day-to-Day Strategies throughout the Season

_____

_____

_____

_____

Post-season Strategies

_____

_____

_____

_____

Reminders

_____

_____

_____

_____

Check-in

Set up your first check-in.

When will the first check-in take place?

_____

How will you assess my progress (for example, self-reflection, observe athletes, talk with athletes, have another person observe me in action)?

_____

_____

_____

_____

_____

_____

Evolve

Consider the following questions:

Celebrate Your Successes: What is going well?

_____

_____

_____

_____

_____

_____

Seek Improvement: What ways can I improve (that is, how can I strengthen the caring and task-involving climate)?

_____

_____

_____

_____

Recognize You Are Doing Your Best and Learn From Your Mistakes: What adjustments can I make (that is, what strategies can you tweak and what strategies do you need to replace)?

_____

_____

_____

_____

Sources

[1]   Gano-Overway, L. A. & Carson Sackett, S. (in press). The Mappway: Success through integration of the motivational and caring climates. *Journal of Applied Sport Psychology.* doi: 0.1080/10413200.2019.1647476

[2]   International Council for Coaching Excellence (ICCE), the Association of Summer Olympic Federations (ASOIF) and Leeds Metropolitan University (2013). *International sport coaching framework.* Champaign, IL: Human Kinetics.

ACKNOWLEDGMENTS

As we have reflected upon our writing of this book, we realize that it would not be possible without the many people in our lives who taught us the importance of creating a caring and task-involving climate and in so doing taught us many life lessons that helped us become better people. We would like to thank them.

Family & Friends

Lori: I would like to thank Daryl Gano for his continued guidance and support over the years as well as helping to instill in me many of the tenets of a caring and task-involving climate (i.e., give your best effort, continue to look for ways to improve, learn from your mistakes, and recognize everyone has good in them); Lisa Booth for being my biggest cheerleader making me keenly aware of the importance of having supportive others in your life as well as reminding me of being present and joyful; Olivia, Victoria, and AJ, as well as Tuffie along with the other Gano-Overway canine companions for their inspiration and showing me the importance of unconditional love and support; Lisa Manhart and Michele Strano for being positive role models in my life for how to share and care; and, most importantly, Ken for being my best friend, exhibiting respect and kindness, and sharing life's journey with me.

Mary: Thanks to Beth and M. L. who created my first caring climate, and to all the members of the Walling/Reedy/Fry clans who make the world a better place every day in all that they do. Thanks also to my besties, Andy, Jared, & Lindsey for bringing joy to my world daily.

Marta: Thanks to Maria Pau for her unyielding love and unconditional support, a pillar in my life and role model of resilience and courage, and to Francesc who always believed in and cheered for me; Sonia, my life-long best friend who always has my back; Agusti for his unwavering positive outlook on life; Elia and Ignasi for becoming tight-knit with us; "Las Pacas" and "Amics de Sempre"— the epitome of an enduring caring climate; my charms: Julia, for pushing me when I give up, Marc, who shows me how to live life as it happens and Sara, who keeps me on my toes; and mostly Jaume, my stalwart of love and support.

Mi-Sook: I would like to deeply thank Ae-Sook who gave me opportunities to see the world and become who I am, and taught me that life is about giving and caring for who I am with.

Maria: I would like to thank all of my students for their inspiration, hard work, and devoted focus to being better scholars and people.

We also would like to thank Michelle Magyar, a dear friend and key contributor in our early research endeavors who helped to form our thinking on the caring climate, and Doris Watson, who helped facilitate our initial research on caring climate.

Coaches

We wrote this book because we believe that coaches make a difference in the lives of others as we have experienced this first hand. Therefore, we would like to recognize the following coaches for helping us reach our potential in athletics AND helping us grow in positive ways as people: Agusti Alvarez, Doug Atkinson, Amy Donnelly, Tina Gaither, Mary Ann Egnatuk, Jan Furman, George Fleming, Ki-Young Kim, Gerard Manoli, Ed Olson, Diccon Ong, Deborah Pittak, Al Riddle, Moses Ruiz, and Barbara Shiery. When we think of the many aspects of the caring and task-involving climate, we think of our experiences with you.

Mentors

Our thinking about the climate, coaching, and life have been shaped by the many individuals who taught us along the way. We are appreciative to the following individuals for their guidance and support over the years: Joan Duda, Peter Anderson, Gloria Balague, Jaume Cruz, Martha Ewing, Diane Gill, Betty Lou Raker, and Jin Yoo.

Students

A heartfelt thanks to all the students who have helped us develop as teachers, mentors, and human beings in this world. We have learned much about caring from all of you. Special shout outs go to members of the KU Sport & Exercise

Psychology Lab and the University of Memphis Sport Psychology Lab for their incredible brain power, passion, and ability to create caring climates.

Contributors to the Writing Process

We offer thanks to Georgette Enriquez from Routledge who first saw potential for our book topic, and to Christina Chronister, Molly Selby, Sara Barnes, Lauren Ellis, and Sarah Green who have seen us through the process. We appreciate Gloria Balague, Gabe Downey, Candace Hogue, and Aubrey Newland for reviewing a draft of the manuscript and providing thorough and helpful feedback that made the book better. We also want to thank Annette Hernandez for her creativity and patience in designing the graphics for the book.

We would also be remiss if we did not acknowledge that this book is a result of our collaborative work with one another. We recognized early on that each one of us came to the group with a set of strengths that helped improve the outcome of each project. Additionally, the love, guidance, kindness, encouragement, and respect exhibited by all members throughout the years meant that we cared for and supported each other when they needed it the most. While we know that this book is better because of our collective efforts we also know our life is better because we share it with one another.

INDEX

Note: Page numbers in *italic* denote figures and in **bold** denote tables.

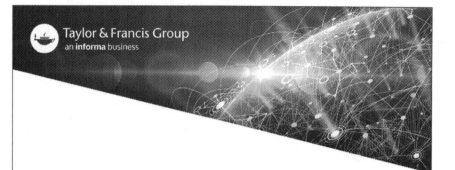

Printed in the United States
by Baker & Taylor Publisher Services